Your baby's
FIRST YEAR

LONDON, NEW YORK, MUNICH, MELBOURNE, DELHI

First American Edition, 2005
Published in the United States by
DK Publishing, Inc.
375 Hudson Street
New York, New York 10014
06 07 08 10 9 8 7 6 5 4

The information in this book was previously published in 2004 within the
following titles in the JOHNSON'S® Everyday Babycare series:

JOHNSON'S® *Breastfeeding*
JOHNSON'S® *Sleep*
JOHNSON'S® *Crying & Comforting*
JOHNSON'S® *Feeding Your Baby*
JOHNSON'S® *Baby & Child Safety*
JOHNSON'S® *Learning to Talk*

A Cataloging-in-Publication record for this book is available from the
Library of Congress.
ISBN-13: 978-0-7566-0936-8
ISBN-10: 0-7566-0936-4

Reproduced by Colourscan, Singapore
Printed in Singapore by Star Standard

Discover more at
www.dk.com

A message to parents from
Johnson's®

The most precious gift in the world is a new baby. To your little one, you are the center of the universe. And by following your most basic instincts to touch, hold, and talk to your baby, you provide the best start to a happy, healthy life.

Our baby products encourage parents to care for and nurture their children through the importance of touch, developing a deep, loving bond that transcends all others.

Parenting is not an exact science, nor is it a one-size-fits-all formula. For more than a hundred years, Johnson & Johnson has supported the healthcare needs of parents and healthcare professionals, and we understand that all parents feel more confident in their role when they have information they can trust.

That is why we offer this book as our commitment to you to provide scientifically sound, professionally reviewed guidance on the important topics of pregnancy, babycare, and child development.

As you read through this book, the most important thing to remember is this: You know your baby better than anyone else. By watching, listening and having confidence in your natural ability, you will know how to use the information you have in your hands, for the benefit of the baby in your arms.

contents

0-3
months

" I didn't realize I'd enjoy caring for Sam so much. We have our **bonding time** together every day. "

SARAH, mother of six-week-old Sam

" Ben is a gorgeous, healthy baby— he **positively glows** with health. I love watching him at my breast and thinking to myself, that's **pure goodness.** "

ELLEN, mother of six-week-old Ben

The benefits of breastfeeding

Breastfeeding will give your baby the best possible start in life. Wherever you are, whatever your circumstances, whether you've given birth to a full-term baby or one who is premature—breastfeeding is a gift that's yours, and yours alone, to give to your child.

Benefits for your baby

Breast milk is the perfect food for your baby because it has been developed and designed over thousands of years with him in mind. No matter how good formula milk is—and it's true to say that it is better now than it's ever been—it can at best only mimic breast milk, and will never be as good as the real thing. Why? Because breast milk is packed with the exact nutrients a human baby needs. It also contains living antibodies from your body that help protect your baby from disease.

For hundreds of years, all over the world, people have understood that breast milk protects babies in addition to helping them grow. Over recent years, doctors and scientists have carried out studies to show exactly how strong the protection offered by breast milk is, and more studies are being carried out all the time. These studies have all reached the same conclusion: Breastfeeding protects your child against illness, both in the first few months of life and during the childhood years beyond.

● Breastfed babies have a far lower risk of gastrointestinal illnesses, which are responsible for the hospitalization of a sizable number of babies every year.

● Exclusive breastfeeding protects against respiratory illness: One study found that babies fed by bottle, or combined breast and bottle, ran twice the risk of getting a lung or respiratory tract infection of some kind.

● Urinary tract infections are less common among breastfed babies; bottle-fed babies were found to have five times the risk of these.

● Ear infections are less common among breastfed babies.

● Studies suggest that breastfeeding also offers some protection against Sudden Infant Death Syndrome (SIDS).

Research results

Studies show that breastfed babies reach their milestones quicker than other babies.

In particular, they seem to:

● learn to crawl earlier

● learn to speak sooner

● have a higher IQ—babies breastfed for between seven and nine months have higher intelligence on average than those breastfed for less than seven months.

Research has also shown that breastfeeding boosts your baby's immune system in ways that give him long-term protection while he's growing up:

- a child who was breastfed is less likely than one who was bottle-fed to get a respiratory illness, up to the age of seven
- there's some long-term protection against gastrointestinal illnesses
- breastfeeding reduces the risk of developing either asthma and eczema
- there's a lower risk of childhood diabetes and leukemia if a baby has been breastfed
- a child who was breastfed is less likely to be obese than one who was bottle-fed.

One study found that children born prematurely seem to benefit from being fed breast milk in the early weeks of life: They had an 8.3 point IQ advantage over premature babies who hadn't been fed breast milk. Full-term babies who'd been breastfed for four months or less had a 3.7 point

ON THE SCALES
Most healthy full-term babies don't need weighing very often: you'll know your baby is feeding well and growing if he is perky and produces plenty of wet diapers.

IQ lead on those who'd been bottle-fed. It's thought that these IQ advantages are due to the long-chain polyunsaturated fatty acids in breastmilk, which are essential for brain development. Other studies have found that breastfed babies tend to crawl and improve their fine motor skills earlier than bottle-fed babies.

Expert tip

Breastfeeding prepares a baby's jaw and mouth muscles for speech. Anecdotally, healthcare professionals report that breastfed babies speak earlier than bottle-fed infants—it is thought that feeding from a nipple strengthens more muscles in the face and jaw than feeding from a bottle.

Will breastfeeding help me bond with my baby?

Breastfeeding a baby is one of the most intimate human experiences: You and your baby are snuggled, tummy to tummy, in a warm and lengthy embrace. It's a wonderful, nature-given opportunity to enjoy being at one with this remarkable little person who's spent so long inside your body. Breastfeeding is the perfect way to bond with your baby.

The love hormone

That isn't to say that women who don't choose to breastfeed don't bond with their babies, or that every feeding will be an idyllic experience. But when breastfeeding is going well, it is undoubtedly a special bonding time with your baby.

Oxytocin, one of the hormones released in the mother during breastfeeding, is known as the "love hormone." Scientists believe that oxytocin primes a new mother to love her baby and to bond with him. It is nature's way of ensuring that new babies are loved and cared for, right from the start.

Make time to bond

Even if you are breastfeeding, bonding won't necessarily happen immediately after birth. Learning to love your baby may take a few hours or days or even weeks. The secret is to learn to relax. Make time to bond. If you're back at home, go to bed with your baby for a day or two and spend some uninterrupted time together if you can. Remember that breastfeeding isn't just about getting enough milk in: It's about pouring love into your baby, too. While you're feeding him, think about how the world looks from his point of view. You are everything to him.

LEARNING HOW TO LATCH ON
Make sure you learn early on how to position your baby correctly and ensure a good latch—this will pay dividends later.

There's no research to suggest that if you don't have a "successful" breastfeeding within a certain time of the birth, your long-term success will suffer. The best advice is to take things easy, relax, and believe that both you and your baby will get the hang of it in time. And you will.

Your hospital stay

There are pros and cons to your hospital stay. On the upside, if you need any help breastfeeding, there are trained nurses all around who will support and advise you. However, if you're in a postnatal ward, you may be surrounded by other new mothers and their babies. This can mean like-minded people to talk to, but it can also mean having to put up with other babies' crying, and lots of people coming and going.

Getting expert advice

It's a good idea to use your hospital stay to get some expert advice on breastfeeding techniques. You may be visited by a lactation consultant as a matter of routine, but if not, ask to see her. And if you have any questions about your baby's feeding and growth that a doctor could help with, make a point of speaking with your healthcare provider as soon as possible after you've been discharged. Many new mothers worry about the

What is colostrum?

Colostrum is the milk your breasts produce during the first few days after the birth; unlike mature milk, which is thinner-looking, colostrum is creamy and thick. It's loaded with protein, a small amount of fat and carbohydrates, and best of all, it's incredibly easy for a baby to digest. So, although you may feel you aren't producing a huge volume of milk, remember that what you are making is full of goodness. Colostrum is also full of antibodies, including some new ones that your baby didn't have access to in the womb.

The first feeding

Studies show that the earlier breastfeeding starts, the easier it's likely to be. If possible, make sure the healthcare professionals who are with you for the birth know you want to be able to put your baby to the breast as soon as possible after she's born. Don't worry if your baby doesn't immediately latch on. It's great if this does happen, but it really doesn't mean you're doomed to failure if she doesn't—far from it. Many babies are simply too interested in the big new world around them to start breastfeeding right away.

amount of milk, or colostrum, they seem to be producing in the early days. It's true that for the first two or three days after the birth, your milk, or colostrum, won't be high in volume, but this is because newborn babies don't need a lot of liquid. They're born with reserves of water—the loss of this is what causes the traditional dip in their weight in the days after birth— but what they really need is the antibody protection of breast milk.

Leaving the hospital

In the hospital you may have had 24-hour help with breastfeeding from medical staff. If you've called on them for support, you may find the idea of leaving to go home daunting. Many women, however, find that breastfeeding gets easier when they're back in their own familiar surroundings.

It's important once you leave the hospital to know where you can go for help and support if you need it. Call an adviser at the first hint of a problem. Get help if you have a tender lump in your breast, you are feeling feverish, or there is a red patch on your breast. These are all signs of a possible blocked milk duct, which could lead to mastitis (see page 21), but if treated right away, it can be stopped.

Your emotions

In the days after the birth, you may feel tired and emotional a lot of the time—common problems can seem overwhelming. This is normal, and almost all mothers can remember going through something similar.

Persevere and try to believe things will improve—it might help to talk to another woman who remembers what everything felt like in the early days. It's important, too, to have the support of someone you trust—perhaps your breastfeeding consultant, midwife, or visiting nurse. Decide whose support you most value and listen to that one person.

Breastfeeding twins

• Beware of people who might be skeptical about your ability to breastfeed two babies. You're perfectly capable of feeding your twins: Breastfeeding works on the supply-and-demand principle, so two babies sucking produces enough milk for both!

• Breastfeeding both the babies together will save you a lot of time. But you'll probably sometimes want to feed them one by one, to help you bond with them individually.

• A good way to feed both is to use the football hold (see right and page 15). Or lay them in front of you with their legs overlapping, making an X-shape in your lap.

• Use lots of pillows so you're comfortable—you may find it worth investing in a V-shaped cushion.

• Alternate feeding each baby from both breasts—this evens out their needs and prevents you from getting lopsided if one baby feeds more than the other.

How do I position my baby?

Good positioning is crucial to happy and contented breastfeeding. Not only does it ensure that you and your baby are comfortable and help you avoid sore nipples, but it also helps the milk to flow properly and your baby to suck more efficiently. Take as much time as you need to make sure your baby is positioned correctly.

CRADLE HOLD
This is the classic breastfeeding position. Make sure your baby's face and entire body are turned toward your breast—her head should be lying on the fleshy part of your arm. Alternatively, you can support her head with your opposite arm.

Latching on

Wait until your baby's mouth is open really wide before you move her close to the nipple, and always bring your baby to your breast, never your breast to your baby. Signs that you've got a good latch include:

★ her lower lip is curled back underneath your nipple

★ your baby's ears move as she sucks

★ you feel no pain at all or only a slight pain as she starts to suck (if it's very painful, take her off the breast and reposition her because a bad latch will cause sore nipples).

Make yourself comfortable

Always make sure you're feeling comfortable before you start breastfeeding. If possible, in the early days, get someone else to hold the baby while you sit down and arrange yourself. Have plenty of cushions or pillows handy—you might like to use them to lay the baby on.

ROOTING
Brush your newborn's upper lip with your nipple to coax her to open her mouth wide enough to get a good latch.

ENSURING A GOOD LATCH
If you are at all unsure about your baby's position or latch, ease her off the breast and start again.

COMING OFF THE BREAST
Slide your little finger into the corner of your baby's mouth to break the seal it forms around your breast.

Once your baby is in position, use your free hand to support your breast and offer it to her. This is especially important in the early days, since your breasts will be full and heavy—latching on will soon become easier and you won't think twice about it, but right now you need to give it your full attention.

Cup your free hand around your nipple in what's called the C hold—this means you'll have your four fingers underneath your nipple and your thumb on top, making the shape of a letter C. Keep your fingers back from the areola, and don't squeeze it too tightly or you may constrict the milk ducts—you're guiding the nipple to your baby's mouth, not squeezing the milk into her.

Different positions

Alternatives to the traditional cradle hold (opposite) include lying down to nurse (right) and the football hold (a good position to try in the early days since it gives you more control over the baby's head).

Women who have had a cesarean section may also find it particularly comfortable since it keeps the baby's weight off the scar. Use a pillow or cushion to support your baby's body, and tuck her torso and legs in under your arm, with her head in your hand.

LYING DOWN TO NURSE
This is a great way to nurse, especially after a cesarean. Lie on your side with your baby facing your breast. Keep her head level with your breast so she doesn't have to pull or reach for your nipple. Her body should be tucked in against your side.

Questions & Answers

My baby is two days old, and my nipples are really sore. What should I do?

You need help getting the positioning right (see pages 14–15). Ask a lactation consultant to give you some advice. If one side is less sore than the other, feed from that side first—once the milk is flowing, the pain will lessen. Expressing a little milk from the sore breast will also help ease the pain.

My breasts are rock-solid and uncomfortable. Why is this?

This is common in the days after the birth—your breasts are over-producing because they don't "know" how much milk your baby needs. Things will settle down in time. Until then, use a warm compress on your breast before feeding—this will help the letdown reflex. Between feedings, use a cold compress or ice pack to help relieve swelling and pain. Some women find that putting a cold, raw cabbage leaf inside their bra helps relieve discomfort.

My milk spurts out so fast that the baby is almost choked by it! Should I be worried by this?

It's quite common to have a lot of milk in the days after giving birth because your body hasn't yet "learned" how much it needs to make, so to compensate, it's overproducing. Things will soon start to settle down over the next few days and weeks.

Back at home

The big plus to stepping over your own threshold with your baby in your arms is that you can finally relax in your own bed with your familiar things all around you. Make the most of it: Pamper yourself, and lap up every bit of pampering offered by your partner.

Breastfeeding works best when you can focus on your baby as much as possible. Obviously, you'll want your partner to be fully involved in the early hours and days with her, but also find quiet times when you can concentrate on nursing your baby.

Later on you'll be able to breastfeed regardless of any commotion, but the process of getting breastfeeding going will be smoother if you're able to devote your attention fully to your baby as you're nursing.

These early days when you're back home are sometimes called your "babymoon" period: It's the time when you can nestle down and simply enjoy being together—you, your baby, and your partner. Friends and family will call and want to rush over to see the baby—but, despite part of you being eager to show her off, try to hold back from too many

BURPING

Burping helps your baby get rid of any air she has taken in while feeding: a rub on the back or a gentle pat is usually all that's needed.

After a cesarean section

If you've had a cesarean section, you may face extra challenges when you start breastfeeding, but there's no reason to think you won't be able to do it. To begin with, both you and your baby may still feel a little woozy from the effects of the drugs you were given, but try to be patient, because when they wear off, your milk will come in and you will soon become as expert at breastfeeding as any other mother.

If your scar is painful in the first few days, try using the relaxation techniques you learned in your prenatal classes.

These positions may also help:
- lying down (see page 15)

- laying your baby on a V-shaped cushion that protects your scar while she feeds

- sitting up in bed—if this isn't too painful—with lots of pillows across your knees to support the baby.

visitors all at once. Remember that you'll have plenty of time in the weeks and months ahead to share this new little person. For the moment, what's crucial for you both—and for your future breast-feeding—is that you take time to focus on one another and on getting breastfeeding right.

Remember to talk to your baby while you're nursing her. Tell her how well she's doing—whisper to her how much you love her. It isn't just milk you are pouring into her little body—it's love as well. And that's every bit as important in helping her to grow big and strong.

How often should I nurse?

It's common to worry about how often and for how long your baby nurses. However, it's best to resist trying to gauge how much milk your baby takes from you.

- Most babies will stop suckling, fall asleep, or just release the breast when they have had enough. Experts do not recommend timing feedings; instead, allow your baby to decide how much she wants by coming off the first breast on her own. Then you can burp her and offer the second side. Some babies will feed 10 minutes per side, others 30. As she feeds longer she will get more of the hindmilk,

which is higher in fat, giving her a feeling of fullness, and she will release the breast or fall asleep.
- Alternate which breast your baby starts on to keep up your milk supply.

Expert tip

It's very important that your baby keeps up her intake of fluids—dehydration is a serious condition in a small baby, and it can take hold very quickly. If your baby stops being interested in nursing, seems floppy, has a dry mouth or eyes, is producing few wet diapers, or has diarrhea or frequent vomiting, get medical help right away.

" Feeding Amy makes me feel really fulfilled right now. I love the way that breastfeeding underlines the fact that she comes first, whatever else is going on. "

CATHERINE, mother of five-week-old Amy

Growing confidence

By the time your baby is four to six weeks old, the early challenges should be behind you, and you and your little one should be breastfeeding easily and happily. His feedings will probably have taken on a broad pattern. They may not be exactly the same every day, but in general you will find that he wants to be fed more and to sleep more, usually in the morning. He gradually has smaller feedings, and longer wakeful periods, as the day wears on.

As time goes by, this pattern will probably evolve further, until his

Is my baby getting enough milk?

This is a common question, and there are plenty of clues as to whether your baby is getting enough milk. Look out for:

● Six to eight wet diapers over a 24-hour period.

● Yellow stools—it doesn't matter if you get several dirty diapers a day or

one every few days; in general, babies older than a month will start to go for longer periods without passing a stool.

● Gradual weight gain, although this doesn't need to be perfectly consistent. A slowdown in weight gain doesn't mean that feeding isn't going well— it's just a temporary dip.

● A baby who is generally alert, bright-eyed, and interested in what's going on around him.

● A feeling of softer, less heavy breasts after your baby has fed.

If these indicators seem to fit you and your baby, you can relax, because breastfeeding is going just fine!

naps consolidate by around the age of seven months into a morning nap and an afternoon nap—one of these, often the morning one, will be longer. You'll find your baby wants to be fed before and often after a nap, although the post-nap feeding may be little more than a pick-me-up, and he'll neglect even that as he grows older.

How many feedings should my baby have each day?

It's sometimes said that the best approach to breastfeeding is not to count your baby's breastfeedings:

Breastfeeding is difficult to quantify, and it's almost impossible to estimate how much milk your baby is taking in. Having said that, research shows that babies tend to have between eight and 12 feedings a day, and doctors sometimes suggest counting a baby's feedings over a 24-hour period to make sure they are in the ballpark. Too many feedings, over a consistent period, may suggest the baby isn't feeding as efficiently as he could; too few feedings could mean he needs to spend more time at the breast to increase his intake.

Growth spurts

Yesterday your baby was blissfully happy—today he wants to be fed all day! He may be having a growth or appetite spurt, so his body needs more milk and communicates that fact to your breasts by sucking more than usual. This "tells" your body to produce more milk, and it will do so in the coming days.

Your body almost certainly can provide enough milk for your baby—you just have to give it a chance. Watch for the signals: When you see your baby needing to suck more often, make sure you give him the opportunity. Don't offer him a bottle or pacifier instead, or you'll keep him from getting the message through to your breasts, and he'll be even more hungry tomorrow.

Talking about your feelings

Being with a small baby all day long is a wonderful privilege—there will be many occasions when you'll look down with love and pride at your growing child and reflect on how far you've come in so short a time.

But looking after a small baby on your own—as many women do—is tiring and sometimes lonely work. Babies are marvelous, but even though you can talk to them all the time (and this is very good for them) they can't chat about the book you're reading or the TV program you watched last night. You need other company sometimes, so if you're usually in the house on your own with the baby during the day, try to find like-minded friends to meet and talk to. Joining or starting a playgroup with a couple of other mothers whose babies are roughly the same age as yours is an excellent way to get much-needed company, support, and advice.

Above all, don't soldier on alone. If you feel you have no energy, if getting up in the morning is a huge hurdle, or if you're finding it difficult to see the meaning or fun in life, you may have postpartum depression. Talk to someone—your partner, your mother, or a healthcare professional. If you are depressed, it may be difficult to put things into perspective, so do seek help.

MEETING NEW FRIENDS
It's useful to join groups or organizations to help find like-minded friends to talk to and who can offer you support and advice if you need it.

Fewer night feedings

Nighttime feedings can be tiring, and cutting them down is high on the wish list of most new moms. You can help reduce feedings by:

• keeping the bedroom dark and interacting with your baby as little as possible when he wakes at night, reinforcing the message that nighttime is when people are quiet and when they go to sleep rather than get up and play

• stroking his back or head rather than lifting him out of his crib when he wakes—he may go back to sleep without a feeding, which will help break the cycle of waking.

Is breastfeeding a contraceptive?

As you continue to breastfeed over the weeks and months after your baby's birth, your period is unlikely to return. What this means is you almost certainly aren't ovulating, so you can't conceive another baby. It's important to realize that you shouldn't rely on breastfeeding as a contraceptive if you really don't want to conceive again right away. But it seems to be the case that if:

• you have not had a period
• your baby is under six months old
• you are breastfeeding exclusively, then you have only a two percent chance of becoming pregnant.

It's nature's way of spacing babies—your body knows that, since your breasts are making milk for your baby's frequent feedings, you've got your hands full, so it gives you a break by stopping ovulation and not conceiving another child too soon.

Some women are happy to let nature take its course if they know they want another baby—what you need to know is that from the time your baby is six months old, you are increasingly likely to become fertile again. However, some mothers who breastfeed go

Troubleshooting

Hopefully you'll sail through breastfeeding without any problems. But just in case, here's what to do if:

• **you get sore nipples**
Reread the section in this book on positioning and latching on (see pages 14–15) because bad positioning is almost always the root cause of sore nipples. Talk to a lactation consultant so you can perfect your technique. Sometimes a simple suggestion will make all the difference. Expressing a little breast milk onto the sore nipple is a good way of relieving the pain.

• **you get one or more tender lumps in your breast**
This may be a blocked duct. Nurse your baby from this side as much as possible, take a warm bath, massage the firm area, and express a little bit of milk while in the tub to get the milk moving through your breast again.

• **you start feeling feverish or have a red spot on your breast**
This could be the start of mastitis or breast inflammation. Nurse as much as possible from the affected breast, get lots of rest, and move your arm on that side to improve blood flow to the area. See your doctor for advice.

• **your baby has suddenly started to refuse the breast**
Your milk may have changed in flavor. Are you on medication? Have you been getting a lot of exercise, causing a temporary buildup of lactic acid in your milk? Has your period restarted, or are you pregnant again? The hormonal changes could be making a difference. Changes to breast milk are usually temporary, and your baby soon starts to nurse again. Another cause of a baby refusing to nurse can be that he has a stuffy nose. If refusing feedings continues beyond two or three feedings, get medical help.

• **you think your baby is comfort–sucking**

If you think your baby is enjoying sucking at the breast, but isn't taking in a lot of milk, it may be that he is actually taking in more than you realize. Or he might be sucking to encourage your breasts to make more milk for tomorrow—upping the demand factor. Alternatively, he might just need to feel close to you right now—and who's to say that's not just as important as getting his milk?

for a year or even two without the resumption of their period.

Most women, however, choose to exercise more control over their fertility. If you fall into this category, talk to your doctor or see a family planning specialist to discuss your needs—the method of birth control you've used in the past may not be appropriate for your current needs.

Birth control pills that contain estrogen are likely to interfere with your milk supply, so the progesterone-only pill is more commonly prescribed, and no studies have shown there to be any harmful effect on the baby. Despite this, some mothers choose not to take oral contraceptives while they're breastfeeding, and for them a barrier method (condoms or a diaphragm) may be the best option. If you decide to use a diaphragm or cervical cap and have used one in the past, you must have a new one fitted now because childbirth changes the size of your cervix.

TEAM EFFORT
By giving his support and helping you while you breastfeed, your partner will quickly become part of the nursing routine.

INVOLVING SIBLINGS

Once you are breastfeeding confidently, talk to older siblings while you feed and try to make sure they don't feel left out.

Your partner's role

Will your partner feel left out because you're breastfeeding your baby? The answer to this is very complex: a mother and her breastfed baby have an extremely close and exclusive relationship and, inevitably, some dads do feel left out. But there are lots of ways in which your partner can support both you and your baby. Specifically, he can spend time cuddling, and then playing with, his child. He can also change diapers, give baths, and do other chores as well.

Your partner can also help you get comfortable when you're preparing to breastfeed, and bring you a glass of water or juice if you need one. He can help you recover from wakeful nights by taking care of the baby in the morning, while you get an extra hour or two of sleep, and he can make sure you eat nutritious meals by shopping for and cooking them.

No dad wants to feel as though he's been usurped by a newborn. Be sensitive to your partner's needs: Like you, he has a whole new way of life to get used to. Perhaps the biggest plus for both of you is that you have one another to share the delight of this new little person.

Checklist

WHAT YOU NEED TO AVOID

● **Alcohol** Studies show that alcohol is dangerous for the developing baby. Women should continue to abstain from alcohol while breastfeeding.

● **Smoking** This can decrease your milk supply. In addition, nicotine is passed on in breast milk. Thinking of your baby and his vulnerability to cigarette smoke is a good motivation for getting you to quit smoking, and you should speak to your healthcare provider about ways of kicking the habit. But if you continue to smoke, don't think you can't breastfeed—your milk is still the best food for your baby, although you should always smoke away from him, preferably outside, or in another room at the very least.

● **Drugs** If you need to take prescribed or over-the-counter drugs for any reason, always tell your doctor or pharmacist that you are breastfeeding.

● **Too much exercise** Heavy workouts can increase the amount of lactic acid in your milk, which may affect the taste, but for most mothers and babies this is not a problem.

● **Certain foods and drinks** You should also avoid caffeine, too much spicy or acidic food, and peanuts if there is a history of peanut allergy in the family.

Can I breastfeed when I'm in public places?

It's normal to feel a little nervous and self-conscious when you first breastfeed in public. What you'll find, however, is that the more you do it, the easier it gets. And it's worth getting used to breastfeeding when you're out because doing so means you'll maximize the benefits—after all, breast milk is the best convenience food ever invented!

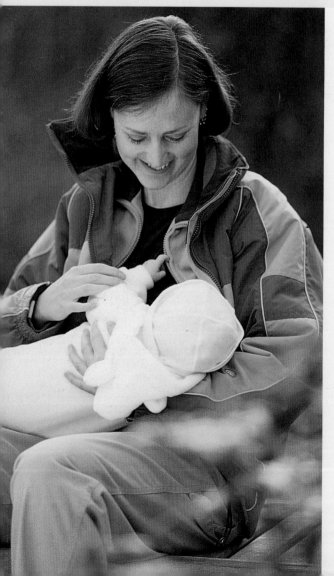

Tips for breastfeeding in public

Get confident about breastfeeding before you do it in front of other people or in a public place—it can be daunting at first, so try to make it as easy and straightforward as possible. Have someone with you—ideally, another breastfeeding mother.

★ Find a place where there are other parents and small children so you'll feel you are among friends.

★ Take a change of clothes for you and your baby.

★ Breastfeeding can make you thirsty, so always carry a bottle of water for yourself in your bag.

★ Wear a sweater or jacket over your top—if your breasts leak, you'll be able to cover it up.

★ If your milk lets down when you aren't ready to nurse, press hard on your breasts with your upper arms—this inhibits the flow.

Breastfeeding rooms

Some stores and shopping malls have breastfeeding rooms where mothers can take their babies to feed them discreetly. Many breastfeeding mothers don't like the idea of being shut away in a little room—

they say no one should be made to feel they have to hide in order to breastfeed. Others feel that they can't breastfeed publicly and, for them, breastfeeding rooms make the difference between being able to go out and having to stay at home.

Baby comes first

Wherever you are and whoever you are with, if your baby needs to nurse, that should come first, and those around you should respect that.

If for any reason you feel uncomfortable, simply excuse yourself and find somewhere you prefer to sit. Remember that the more breastfeeding mothers choose to feed their babies in public, the more accepted and "normal" this will become.

It's also important to know that breastfeeding can be discreet—often those sitting around you won't notice, especially when you become more adept. And as a breastfeeding mother the law is usually on your side if you choose to nurse your baby in public. Many people will show support for you if they happen to notice you're nursing your baby: if you attract any attention at all, it's more likely to be positive than negative.

EASY DISCRETION

Pulling a top up from the waist to breastfeed in public will attract less attention than unbuttoning a shirt. It's also a good idea to carry a light shawl with you in case you feel the need for extra cover.

CAREFUL POSITIONING

If you're in a restaurant, choose a seat facing away from other customers—this will make you feel less self-conscious as you nurse. More than likely, the people sitting around you won't even notice that you are breastfeeding.

" I can feel my heartbeat quickening when I hear Alexa crying. It really does **trigger** a strong reaction. I need to respond to her and find ways of **calming her down. "**

GINA, mother of nine-month-old Alexa

Crying in young babies

Imagine for a moment what life might be like if your baby never cried. You would have no way of knowing that he was hungry, ill, in pain, or simply needed a hug. Crying is an important part of your baby's survival mechanism. It's a signal that is virtually impossible for parents to ignore, and a highly effective way of ensuring that you will quickly respond to his needs, whatever they happen to be.

The significance of crying

Your baby's cry is designed to grab your attention. When you hear it, your body produces stress hormones that increase your blood pressure and heart rate, and tense your muscles. You become very eager to stop the crying.

Crying also promotes "attachment"—the way in which you bond with your baby when love grows between you. It does this by ensuring that you keep your baby close to you and provide him with plenty of loving attention. Indeed, research has found that babies who have formed a poor emotional attachment to their parents may sometimes cry inconsolably to get the attention they desperately need.

At first, crying is also your baby's main "language" for expressing his needs. Then, as other ways of communicating (especially speech) develop, you will notice that your baby cries less because he doesn't need to rely on crying as a way of making himself understood. Having said that, he will continue to cry throughout childhood, and adulthood, to signal distress.

Patterns and peaks

Your baby cries most during the first three months, after which the rate of crying tends to drop to about half its earlier level. Some babies naturally cry more than others, and there is evidence that these *relative* amounts of crying continue until about one year of age. This means that babies who cry more than others in the first three months are likely to still be crying more at the age of one, even though they are crying less than they were. Perhaps surprisingly, your

How long do babies cry?

Most babies cry on average for approximately:

- two hours a day in the first three months
- one hour a day in the 4-to-12-months period.

Remember, these are *average* figures. Many babies cry more than this, so don't worry if yours seems to be one of them. Interestingly, studies of non-Western communities where there is more frequent body contact and demand feeding suggest that babies there seem to cry less.

Questions & Answers

My three-month-old baby can be very happy, gurgling at her mobile or listening to music one minute, then quite suddenly she starts screaming and goes into a meltdown. Why is this?

It is likely that your baby is showing you that she has become overstimulated. When this happens, move her to a more peaceful area away from too many toys, sights, and sounds. You can try to spot this coming from her body language—she may turn her head away or squeeze her eyes shut, for example, before the crying frenzy starts.

baby's level of crying is not at its highest when he is a newborn. The rate of crying gradually increases from birth until a baby is around six weeks old, then subsides. This pattern is often referred to as the developmental crying peak.

In the first three months, evening crying makes up about 40 percent of the daily total, and about half of all parents report an evening crying peak—usually early evening (see pages 42–45).

Between the ages of about nine and 12 months, nighttime crying

becomes more common, although again, this is often a pattern shown by babies who have been excessive criers up until then.

Coping with change

There is considerable evidence to show that a lot of what causes your baby to cry during the first few months is simply developmental, and/or reflects the need for a

THE FIRST CRY
Your baby's first cry announces that he is taking his first breaths, and is missing the security of the womb.

Sensitive babies

Some babies can be shown to have a low sensory threshold—in other words, they are more sensitive than other babies. They seem to miss the safety of the womb and are easily overwhelmed by new experiences. You can probably recognize this if your baby is one who dislikes being bathed or undressed. Typically, sensitive babies tend to:
- change more rapidly from one behavior state to another—for example, from sleeping to crying
- be easily startled more often
- more frequently tense or jerk their arms and legs.

Sensitive babies may cry as a result of food passing down through their digestive system, having gas, and even from the physical feelings of their own bodies, such as the movement of their arms and legs.

External sensations may be too much for these babies. Sounds, light, smells, faces suddenly coming too close to them, and even being picked up and held, especially by a number of different people, can be upsetting.

If you recognize your baby as being of a sensitive nature, he will enjoy calm, peaceful surroundings and careful handling.

Checklist

To help interpret your baby's needs, think of his crying as a graded signal, the level of which represents increasing distress.

- **Intensity** Consider how loud the crying is. Does the intensity decrease when you hold your baby?

- **Constancy** Note how long your baby's crying lasts. Does it stop when you hold him?

- **Pattern** Note also when the crying occurs. Is it mainly in the morning, afternoon, evening, or night? Before, during, or after feedings? Is it every day, or more on weekdays than on weekends? Is it when he misses a nap, or after being handled a lot or being exposed to a stimulating environment?

- **Length of crying** How many hours a day does your baby's crying last, on average?

consistent, predictable daily routine. From birth, your baby goes through huge changes, physically, socially, and psychologically. It's normal for him to have bouts of persistent crying before a particular developmental stage. This may be connected to major changes in his brain and nervous system when a new developmental challenge is met.

This means that all babies will cry a certain amount, no matter what you do to try to soothe them. So it is not always helpful to think that "something's wrong" or to wear yourself out trying to find solutions to stop the crying.

Excessive crying

Excessive crying is defined as more than three hours of crying in a 24-hour period. As many as one in four babies, from newborn to three months, display this level of crying. Many theories of why babies cry excessively have been tested by researchers but have proven to be unfounded. These include overfeeding or underfeeding, gas pain, "colic" (see pages 42–45), the mother's age, the sex of the baby, allergies, the parents' IQ or educational level, whether they are first-time parents, spoiling, and even whether the baby's mother smoked or drank coffee during pregnancy.

Your baby's temperament

Some babies are more "challenging" than others, and it is simply in their temperament to cry more. It is worth considering that your baby may need a very high level of care and closeness for a while to aid his development, and that crying is a vital, if rather extreme, way to ensure he gets the necessary attention. Even if you have a challenging baby, remember that:

- your baby's crying is *never* his "fault"
- it's certainly not your fault, either
- it does not mean that your child will grow up to be difficult or bad-tempered.

There is no evidence that excessive crying has any effect on development or behavior beyond the first year. He *will* grow out of this stage.

WHAT'S HIS TEMPERAMENT?
He may be active, sensitive, easily overstimulated, or a bit of everything. Getting to know him will help you comfort him.

Sensing your tension

It has been suggested that a baby can pick up on a parent's tension. You may find that even though you try your best to soothe your crying baby, someone else—your partner, a healthcare professional, or a friend— can calm him down more easily.

As a new mother, you may find this very disheartening. You may even start to think that your baby doesn't like you. It is only too easy to feel rejected when your baby seems to dislike being held, or thrashes and cries when you try to carry him in a baby carrier.

While it is tempting to think that you must be doing something wrong, the likelihood is that, because of your emotional bond with your baby, you are feeling so upset by the crying that you are becoming tense and irritable. Your baby senses this tension in you and cries even more. Thus, a vicious circle begins. Make the most of others' offers of help— and if they can soothe your baby in the process, so much the better!

What those cries could mean

Research may not support the theory that a baby's cries sound different depending on his needs, but many parents believe that they can identify several types of crying from their babies—for example, hunger, pain, or irritability—and this helps them try to find ways to soothe them.

- **Hunger** In the early days, hunger is most likely to be the main reason for your baby's cries. It is the most obvious and easiest to deal with. A hunger cry is very persistent and is unlikely to stop until your baby is fed.

- **The need for attention** A baby who needs your attention and probably wants a cuddle may sound fussy.

- **Pain or fright** If your baby is in pain or has been startled by something, his cries are likely to be a very sharp yell.

- **Illness** Although this is rarely the reason that he's crying, a sick baby's cry may be unusual in some way—more high-pitched, for example.

"No matter what is causing Joseph's crying, he loves being held up against my shoulder while I rub his back."

CHRISTINA, mother of nine-week-old Joseph

Questions & Answers

I had a long, difficult labor, and eventually a forceps delivery. My son is now five weeks old and seems hard to comfort. Does his birth experience have anything to do with it?

It's true that some babies may cry more following a complicated delivery or obstetric intervention, such as a forceps, vacuum extraction, or Cesarean delivery.

Also, premature babies, or babies who have spent time in special care, may cry more and need especially sensitive care. It could be that they are experiencing more discomfort or pain, or it may just be that they find it harder to cope with new sights and sounds because of their immaturity.

Consider also the effect the birth may have had on you. A negative experience can cause mothers to take less pleasure in their babies, who may then cry more. A baby who is hard to console can in turn increase a mother's feelings of inadequacy, which makes the situation worse. Talk this through with your healthcare provider, who can offer advice and make sure your baby is well.

Emotional discomfort

All babies need the comfort and reassurance of being held close as often as possible in the early days. If you have ruled out all the potential physical causes of your baby's crying (see bottom right), she probably needs soothing.

● **Insecurity** Your baby may settle down quite happily in your arms or a baby carrier, then be fussy when put down. This is a clear sign that she wants to be near you.

● **Boredom** As your baby gets older, from around five months, she could be crying because she is bored and wants something—or someone—to amuse her. This could happen sooner if she's an active, wakeful baby.

● **Overstimulation** Too much handling, noise, or even play can make your baby irritable and fussy.

● **Overtiredness** An overtired baby needs calm handling. To help relax her and soothe her so that she's able to go to sleep, try gentle rocking, singing, cuddling, stroking, or sitting with her in a quiet, darkened room.

CLOSE TO YOU
Your newborn baby loves the security of your arms, feeling the rhythm of your heartbeat, and gazing into your smiling face.

Adjusting to the world

Newborn babies must make a big adjustment in the first few days of life outside the womb. For some babies, the shock to their senses caused by this arrival is probably just too much, and they express their feelings of discomfort by crying vigorously due to the many unfamiliar sensations of light, noise, and sometimes even the touch of many different people.

In the early weeks, a lot of your baby's crying probably happens simply because you have not yet learned what she likes and dislikes. This takes time and careful attention to all your baby's vocalizations and behavioral communication cues.

Physical discomfort

There are many physical reasons why your baby could be crying:

● **Hunger** As soon as your baby feels hungry, she will cry to be fed. Before she starts to cry, look for early hunger signs, such as rooting, sucking, and even opening and closing her hands over her chest.

● **Thirst** Newborns usually do not need extra fluids, other than their normal feedings. If your baby seems thirsty, offer cooled boiled water or bottled water between feedings.

● **A dirty or wet diaper** While needing a diaper change may not

Spend time observing your baby. This helps you to get to know her and understand her needs. Try not to compare her with other babies. It's important to remember that:

- some babies prefer quiet, still times and very gentle handling, while others want more activity
- some take heartily to feeding; others find it a struggle for a while
- some can be put down easily after feeding; others will always complain and cry
- some babies may need to cry more to ensure that their higher demands for contact and care are met—remember that crying is also an attachment-promoting behavior.

If your baby does seem to cry a lot, it is even more important to make the most of times when she is content by observing and interacting with her. This will help increase the emotional bond between you and your child.

Your personality

If you are a naturally calm person, you may be better able to cope with crying than a more stressed parent would be. This is why individual parents' interpretations of crying vary; one may describe as excessive and unbearable crying that another finds challenging but possible to cope with.

Your home life

Your personal circumstances will also have an impact on how easy it is for you to manage a crying baby. If you have the support of a partner, the experience of having had other children, or friends or family who can share the load with you, then you will probably manage more easily than a single or first-time mother with few friends or relatives living nearby.

If you are on your own, find out about mother-and-baby groups in your area—you will find the friendship and support you receive from meeting other mothers to be an invaluable lifeline.

make every baby cry, leaving your baby in a wet or soiled diaper can aggravate her delicate skin.

- **Gas** Gas can be uncomfortable. Keep her as upright as possible during feedings, and "burp" her by holding her against your shoulder and rubbing or patting her back.

- **Feeling too hot or too cold** Young babies are not able to regulate their own temperature and need your help to make them feel comfortable. To check whether your baby is too hot or too cold, feel her tummy, not her hands or feet. Take off or add extra layers accordingly. Always remove extra

clothing from her when you come into a warm environment, even if she is asleep.

- **Needing a change of position** Before she can shift her position by herself, your baby may cry for help if she is lying uncomfortably. Remember, however, that you must always lay her down to sleep on her back to avoid the risk of Sudden Infant Death Syndrome (SIDS).

How can I comfort my newborn baby?

As you react to your baby's cry, your first thoughts are "Why is she crying?" and "How can I soothe her?" If there's no obvious physical cause (see page 33) for her crying, she'll need your help to calm down. Find out which comforting method works best for your baby and repeat it systematically. If one thing doesn't work, try several together—it's a process of trial and error.

Cuddling, contact, and bonding

★ **Rocking in your arms** Research has shown that your heartbeat, rhythmical breathing pattern, and regular movements help to establish a baby's own regular heart rate and respiratory and sleep patterns. You may find that you instinctively sway your hips whenever you hold your baby close.

A DIFFERENT APPROACH
Don't worry if a tried-and-true method of soothing your baby doesn't seem to work. It's worth persevering with other ways of comforting her until you find one she can't resist.

TENDER LOVING CARE
Your warm embrace will usually prove to be irresistible to your newborn, helping her feel secure, loved, and confident that you are there to meet her needs.

FEELING BETTER
As you rock her in your arms or hold her against your shoulder, watch for signs that her crying is subsiding and that she's ready to drop off to sleep.

★ **A baby carrier** Having your baby in a carrier provides comfort, closeness, and the sensation of movement. It also leaves your hands free.

★ **Stroking** Gentle stroking of the forehead, or anywhere on your baby's body, may help her relax.

★ **Massage** This is the perfect way to soothe and bond with your baby (see pages 40–41). Soft stroking and massage is easy to do, and both you and your baby will benefit from the intimacy.

Other ways to comfort

★ **Sounds and music** Anything from lullabies to pop songs can help. Also try recordings of womb sounds, or "white noise," such as the monotonous hum of the washing machine or vacuum cleaner.

★ **Going for a ride** You may rock your baby when she's in her buggy or cradle and discover that she quiets because of the movement. Taking her out for a walk in her buggy or stroller, or a ride in the car, may also be effective for this reason. However, make sure your baby doesn't come to rely on this as a way of getting to sleep—she needs to learn to do this by herself.

Nursing and crying

In the early weeks, it is normal for your baby to want to feed frequently; every two hours is not unusual. Small preterm babies may need to feed even more often than this to catch up on their growth. Often they are awake more at night and want to sleep all day.

There are several reasons why your newborn needs frequent feedings:

- Breast milk is perfect food for your newborn, but it is low in fat and protein, so she digests it quickly and easily and is soon hungry again.

- Your newborn has a tiny stomach, so "little and often" is best for her.

- It takes time for both you and your baby to learn how to nurse efficiently.

- Remember also that breastfeeding works on a "supply-and-demand" basis, so that as your baby sucks, your breasts are stimulated to make

" We both get so much out of breastfeeding. It helps me relax, and I know I'm giving him the best possible start. "

MELISSA, mother of 12-week-old Daniel

more milk for the next feeding. To keep up with demand, ensure that you eat a nutritious diet and drink plenty of fluids. This is especially important when you feel you need to increase your milk supply.

• Trying to nurse your newborn baby by the clock will inevitably lead to a lot more crying, since it takes several weeks for her feedings to settle into a routine.

Sleeping and crying

In the beginning, your baby doesn't really know the difference between night and day, and it is better to accept your baby's rhythms and routines for now. Trying to fit your baby into an imaginary schedule at this stage will lead to more crying.

Helping your baby

After the first few months, however, it is worth thinking about sleep routines, and you can begin to set up bedtime rituals, such as a bath, a cuddle, and a story in the evening. These are signals that even tiny babies start to recognize.

Even for daytime naps, by about four months it is worth putting your baby down at set times, and in a recognizable way if you can, preferably in the crib in her room.

Sleep facts

It is important to remember that:

• A baby's internal body clock is not fully developed until at least six weeks.

• Babies' sleep patterns are quite different from those of adults. They spend much longer in light, active REM (rapid-eye-movement) sleep when they are more likely to wake—50 percent of the time versus 25 percent in adults.

• Premature babies spend even more time in light sleep.

• It is not until six months or later that a baby's brain regulates sleep in a way similar to an adult's.

The benefits of swaddling

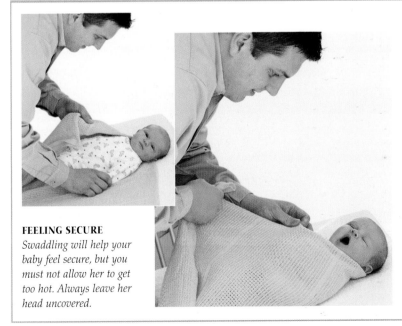

FEELING SECURE
Swaddling will help your baby feel secure, but you must not allow her to get too hot. Always leave her head uncovered.

Wrapping your newborn quite firmly, "papoose-style," in a light blanket or sheet can help to calm her, especially if she's sensitive and easily startled. Many babies are upset by the jerking movements of their limbs, and swaddling stops this from happening.

Fold the blanket or sheet and lay your baby on top of it. Her neck should be level with the fold. Bring one side of the blanket over her body and tuck it firmly under her. Then do the same with the other side. Tuck the end of the blanket under her feet and legs. You may wrap her arms, or leave them free so that she can get her hands to her mouth to soothe herself.

Checklist

When it feels as though your young baby's crying is getting the best of you, take a break (see pages 46–47). The following facts may help you put things into perspective:

- It is not possible to spoil a baby by going to her when she cries.

- Your newborn is never just "exercising her lungs."

- Her crying is a reflex to express needs or to get help when she can't cope alone with the overwhelming changes in her world.

- Your newborn never cries to manipulate you. She is using the only language she has at the beginning to ensure that her needs are met.

Meeting her needs—fast!

There is a great deal of evidence that the more quickly you can respond to your baby's cries in the early days by going immediately to soothe her, the more you will help build a feeling of greater security and confidence. As a result, your baby is less likely to cry excessively later on. There is also a developmental reason for not leaving your newborn to cry for too long.

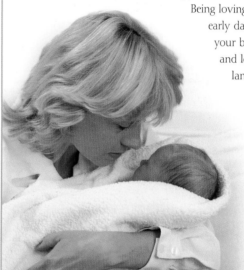

Being loving and responsive in the early days can actually help your baby's brain develop, and lead to better language development. However, many babies do fuss or cry for a short time when first put down, so you may need to leave her for a few minutes to settle down—but never more than five minutes for a new baby.

Take a realistic view

It helps if you have a realistic view of what having a baby is really like. This can be difficult when we see images everywhere of perfectly contented, smiling babies, being cared for by parents who appear to be totally relaxed and confident in their roles. Some parents may have had no chance to learn that, although the reality may sometimes match this rosy picture, there will also be many challenges to face.

The attitude of others may not help the assumption that a "good" baby doesn't cry, and a "good" parent can always solve crying. Neither of these statements is true.

If you are becoming very upset by your new baby's crying, someone less emotionally involved, such as your partner, may possibly be able to soothe her more easily. Remember that this is not a reflection on you—your baby's behavior does not mean you are a bad mother, nor does it mean she doesn't like you. She can react to your tension, so you must share the care and find ways to relax.

Involving dads

Research shows many benefits when dads are fully involved with the day-to-day care of their babies. Their emotional support in the early days is vital, and will make a big difference to you, especially while you are getting breastfeeding established successfully.

Your partner can also play a key role in the early emotional development of your baby. He will create loving bonds by carrying out all the same physical and emotional care that you do.

It's also important that you involve your partner right from the beginning. Not only will his help give you a break; it also stops him from feeling that he's missing out on caring for your baby or that you are so involved with her that you no longer have any time left for him.

Even if you are breastfeeding your baby, there are many other ways your partner can get involved. He can still cuddle, burp, bathe, change diapers, and comfort her when she's crying. He can carry her in a baby carrier, and take her out for a walk in the stroller. Dads are just as capable of doing all the practical babycare activities as you are, and can be equally hands-on parents. The more opportunities they have to hold and cuddle their babies, the more confident and relaxed they become, and the closer their bond. Everyone gains from it.

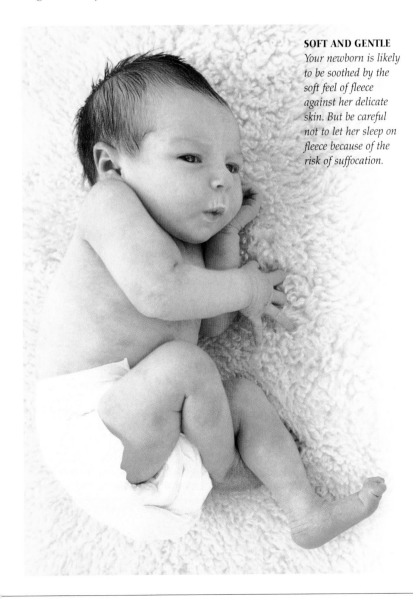

SOFT AND GENTLE
Your newborn is likely to be soothed by the soft feel of fleece against her delicate skin. But be careful not to let her sleep on fleece because of the risk of suffocation.

Self-comforting

Sucking is the most obvious source of comfort for all crying babies. Your newborn can suck the breast, a bottle, or a pacifier, or you can help her to try to find her own fist or your clean fingers. Although it is well known that babies suck their thumbs in the womb, it will be two or three months before they really learn to suck their thumbs effectively.

Can massage help ease my baby's crying?

Baby massage can be relaxing and beneficial for both babies and parents. Through eye contact and touch, it promotes bonding and boosts your baby's confidence and well-being. There is even evidence that it can reduce crying levels and relieve "colic," encourage better sleep patterns, and possibly help boost your baby's immune system. Massage is generally recommended for healthy full-term babies. It is also better not to massage your baby if she seems ill or has had a recent immunization. Baby massage classes are an ideal way to learn the techniques—and to make new friends.

Massaging tips

★ You can massage your baby when she's undressed or through her clothes.
★ Make sure that the room is warm.
★ Your hands should be clean and warm. You may like to use baby oil (avoid aromatherapy or nut-based oils).
★ Pay attention to your baby's cues that she is enjoying the massage. Some babies find it stimulating; others like only one part of their body massaged.
★ Massage is best in between feedings, not just after or just before one.

HEAD AND SHOULDERS
Using the tips of your fingers or thumb, gently stroke your baby's forehead out to her temple, then her neck to her shoulders. If she's alert, keep eye contact, talk softly, and smile at her.

LEGS

Making small circular strokes with your fingertips, or gently squeezing with your hand, massage down from her thighs to her knees, and then down her shins to her ankles. You can work one leg at a time or both simultaneously.

HANDS AND ARMS

From her shoulders, continue your strokes down along her arm to her hand. Again, you can work on one limb at a time or both together. Next, try some very gentle circular strokes on her tummy, using one hand.

FEET

Working down her legs, massage her ankles, her feet, and finally each of her toes. You can finish by gently cycling her legs.

Questions & Answers

Is colic the same thing as excessive crying?

Excessive crying may not fit the patterns and definitions of colic. It can last longer than three months, and may not follow the evening peak pattern. It happens at different times of day, or occasionally lasts for what seems like all day—or all night. Help your baby by starting to establish a sleep/wake routine, so that his world is structured and predictable and to avoid overtiredness. Give him sensitive care according to his temperament, and try to intercept before crying starts.

Excessive crying

Also known as "colic," this is a distressing pattern of crying, usually peaking in the evening, that is at the high end of the spectrum of normal crying, and is something babies "do," rather than something they "have." Colic is not an "illness" in itself, and in the vast majority of cases there is no underlying medical cause. However, it is important to consult your healthcare provider if you are worried about your baby, so he or she can rule out any health problems and reassure you that your baby is well.

Unexplained and inconsolable crying is unusual in that it does not fit well with the idea that babies cry in order to have a need met. You may try everything, and yet your baby still cries.

Also, it has been shown that, despite crying excessively, babies usually do not experience certain

COMFORTING HOLD
A baby with colic may be soothed by being held in a position that allows gentle pressure on her abdomen.

What are the causes?

There have been many unproven theories in the past about what may be the cause of colic, from food intolerances and parental tension to gas pains and evening hunger in breastfed babies. The current thinking about colic crying gives the following possible explanations:

• your baby may have an immature nervous system, especially if she seems very reactive to external factors—lights, sounds, or activities going on around her

• she may be a sensitive baby, needing to cry to block out other distressing sensations

• crying at the end of the day may be your baby's way of releasing tension

• she is having difficulty regulating her behavior and once she starts crying, she doesn't know how to stop—she needs your help to settle down (see pages 44–45)

• it's all down to your baby's temperament—some babies simply cry more than others.

" Scott has just turned three months old and his colic is completely gone. He is much more cheerful, and easier to settle. We can relax in the evenings now!"

GEMMA, mother of three-month-old Scott

Expert tips

Try the following when you are coping with a colicky baby:

• Take turns with your partner caring for your baby, and get as much help and support as possible from friends and relatives to give yourself a break.

• Try to identify a pattern to the crying, by keeping a diary (see page 48). It can help you feel more in control and is also useful for your healthcare providers.

• Talk to other parents who have been through the same experience or call a helpline (see page 156–157).

• Keep reminding yourself that colic lasts for a relatively short period. It is not worth getting too upset or worn out trying to find "cures."

• Focus on every positive moment with your baby. Keep a diary of these too, so you can see that there are good times as well as bad.

physiological changes that might be expected. Their heart rates and levels of cortisol (a chemical in the blood that indicates stress) may remain within the normal range, even when they are crying their hardest!

This type of crying could be considered very similar to sleep difficulties, in that it is a problem, *but not for your baby*. It is the effect these behaviors have on you, her parents, that is the real issue.

Medical concerns

In the past, it has been suggested that colic could be the result of a problem with a baby's immature central nervous or gastrointestinal system. Feeding difficulties, or perhaps a dietary intolerance of some kind (for instance, to cow's-milk protein) have also been put forward as possible causes.

Recent research has concluded, however, that it would be in only a small minority, possibly about 10 percent of cases, that digestive problems could cause this extreme form of crying. Yet parents are often told, as the first response, to change their method of feeding.

However, colic occurs more or less equally in bottle-fed and breastfed babies, so any change would have an effect on only a small number of babies with colic.

Waiting it out

Remember that *all* crying decreases after three or four months. Even though babies who are excessive criers may continue to cry more than other babies until at least five months, they will be crying much less than before.

Also, rest assured that a baby with colic will not become a more difficult toddler or child.

How can I comfort a baby with colic?

Even though you try your best to keep a positive attitude throughout your baby's extreme crying bouts and fervently hold on to the fact that it will end in a few weeks, you probably feel happier trying something—anything!—to comfort your baby, if only for a short while.

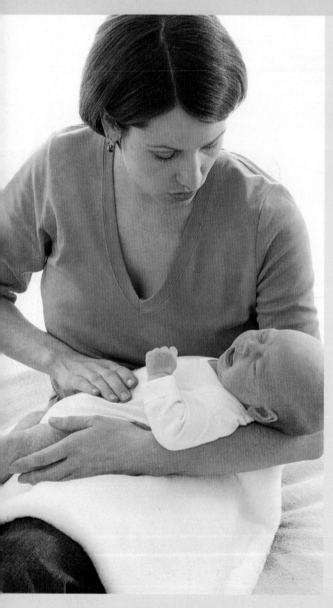

Physical contact

Remember, babies who have more physical contact may cry less. The benefits of cuddling and stroking have a well-proven physiological basis, and even when your baby's crying is not soothed, you may be boosting her immune system and growth hormones. Physical contact is always worthwhile.

It's also worth trying all the usual comfort tips for crying, such as sucking, rocking, playing music or singing, and massage (see pages 40–41). They may help for a while—but don't be surprised if, after a brief lull, your baby starts crying again. Find the three to five most successful strategies and rotate through them in the same order.

GENTLE PRESSURE ON HER TUMMY
Holding your baby in the crook of your arm, place your hand on your baby's tummy and rub it gently. At the same time, maintain eye contact and talk to her softly, using her name regularly.

Soothing techniques

If your baby is not calmed by cuddling, rocking, or stroking, there are other comforting techniques you can try which may ameliorate her crying. These techniques include:

★ doing a "colic dance," in which you rock your baby up and down while swaying your hips from side to side

★ applying gentle pressure to your baby's tummy

★ holding your baby in positions that allow pressure on her abdomen—for example, over your knees, across the crook of your arm, or upright against your shoulder

★ applying warmth to your baby's tummy, such as the gentle heat from a covered hot-water bottle filled with warm—not hot—water held against her through her clothes

★ giving her a bath, but be sensitive to your baby's temperament—some babies with colic find a bath soothing, while others are more agitated by it

★ burping your baby—try keeping her as upright as possible during feedings, or take a break from a feeding, hold her against your shoulder, and gently rub her back to help her bring the gas up.

FACE DOWN
Holding your baby in the crook of your arm allows you to apply gentle pressure to her tummy while swaying her from side to side. She'll feel secure because her body is supported along the length of your arm, and the movement may also distract and soothe her.

PAT HER BACK
When you feel confident with this position, and have a secure hold on the thigh of the leg farthest from your body, use your free hand to pat gently or rub her back using circular movements.

Checklist

Help your other children by:

- encouraging them to talk about their feelings

- sympathizing with them about how distracting the crying can be, reassuring them that this period will not last very long and that soon you will have more time for them again

- thinking of ways to give them undivided attention—perhaps your partner could play with your toddler more, or you could settle down to read to her while you feed the baby

- involving your children as much as possible in helping to amuse or calm the baby—turn it into a family project

- accepting all offers of help—a trip to the movies with a grandparent or a sleepover with a friend will be a welcome treat for older children.

❝ My older children have been so helpful, which is good because I find the more time I can spend comforting Orin, the more relaxed we all are. ❞

FRAN, mother of two-week-old Orin

A baby in the family

As your family grows, you may find yourself with a baby, a demanding toddler, and a child just starting school. You now have a diverse set of relationships to manage, as well as your baby's crying. You may have to explore a range of solutions in order to maintain some of the essential activities of your normal family routine. It is important for all of you to hang on to the fact that these changes in family dynamics are to be expected for a while, and that things will soon return to normal.

When a baby arrives, it's a time of very mixed emotions. Younger children may be quite upset by the idea that the baby may be feeling sad. Older children may find that it interferes with their routines and feel that they are missing out on a good

Getting help

Never be afraid to ask for help, and accept all offers from your partner, grandparents, other family members, or friends.

- Talk to other parents—they have all been there! Find out if there are any postnatal groups you can join in your area.
- Talk to your healthcare professional for general advice and support—particularly if you feel you're beginning to find it hard to cope.
- Look on the Internet for parent support groups, or see *Useful contacts* on pages 156–157.

deal of their parents' attention. All siblings may be annoyed or even angry at the many challenges a new baby brings. But then they are also likely to feel guilty about, or be unable to understand, these negative thoughts.

Be positive

You will inevitably have some guilty moments over how your older children's lives have changed with the arrival of a new baby, and feel yourself pulled in all directions. But don't allow guilt to take away the time your baby needs from you to feel secure. The more you are able to respond to your baby, allowing him to claim your attention so that you learn how to soothe him, the less he will cry in a few months and the happier everyone in the family will be. Always remember that your baby's crying is not your fault, and that it is not a reflection on your abilities as a parent either.

Be confident

The best type of help you need at the moment is from someone who can provide practical support, giving you a break by taking the baby for a while, or emotional support as a nonjudgmental listener.

Expert tips

- Be as honest as you can about how the baby's crying is making everybody feel. It can be hard to express negative thoughts, because the social pressures are so great to pretend that everything is perfect when a new baby arrives. But it can really help everybody to feel relieved that these thoughts and feelings are normal and will pass.

- Consider separate beds or bedrooms for a while so that you and your partner each have the much-needed chance to catch up on sleep and rest. Take turns spending nights with the baby—obviously, you won't have this option if you are breastfeeding, unless you express some milk, but even a few hours of unbroken sleep can be restful.

- Talk things through with your family, and draw up lists of what absolutely needs to be done, and who can do what. Older children may surprise you with their sensible suggestions and offers of help.

- Ask older children to help you keep a diary of your baby's crying (see page 48). Being given the task will make them feel important, and you may all be amazed to find that the crying lasts for less time than you thought.

- Keep your sense of humor—just making a funny face and saying to your toddler, "Oh, no, here we go again!" when the baby starts to cry may lighten everybody's mood.

The crying paradox

In one way, nature seems to have slipped up. Crying is obviously meant to elicit the care needed for survival, ensuring loving interaction and adequate nutrition from parents. Yet, when it goes on and on, it can become "aversive." Studies show that some parents feel angry and less sympathetic toward a baby who cries excessively. If you experience this, you will need help and support. Don't feel guilty—no one has infinite patience. Recognizing that you need help is a positive step. Consult your healthcare provider or call a help line.

Seeking medical advice

Much research has shown that illness is a cause for crying in only a very small percentage of cases. Nevertheless, it is worth consulting your healthcare provider, who can make certain that there are no underlying medical conditions or health problems, and reassure you that your baby is fine.

It will be helpful to you and to your healthcare provider if you keep a diary of your baby's crying for a week or two. Armed with this information, the healthcare provider will be better able to understand your concerns. Your diary should make note of:

• the average number of hours your baby cries per day

• the number of days a week that her crying is a problem

• the intensity of the crying

• the constancy of the crying

• the pattern of the crying throughout the day (such as after a feeding)

• anything that seems to make the crying better or worse.

Minor conditions

There are a number of minor conditions that may make your baby cry. Again, your healthcare provider

KEEPING A CRYING DIARY
A diary is a useful record for your healthcare provider, as well as a reassurance that your baby's crying may not be as persistent as it seems!

can advise you on the best course of action to take to help her.

• **Colds and coughs** A blocked nose may cause your baby to cry in frustration when nursing, since she won't be able to breathe properly. Also, stuffiness and an irritating cough may keep her awake at night, making her overtired and leading to crying. Ask your pharmacist to recommend over-the-counter saline nose drops.

• **Diaper rash** A sore bottom may cause your baby to cry every time she wets her diaper. Change her diaper frequently, letting the air get to her skin, and use a barrier cream to protect her.

● **Thrush** Oral thrush is a fungal infection that can often make feeding painful. Look for white patches inside her mouth, which will not come off if you gently wipe them with a clean handkerchief. Your healthcare provider may prescribe medication.

● **Teething** Once your baby starts cutting her teeth, she may experience some discomfort until a tooth breaks through her gum.

● **Urinary tract infection** This can be hard for parents to spot in babies, although there may be a fever as well as more crying than usual. An older child may pass urine more frequently and the urine may be cloudy or smelly. Your healthcare provider will test your child's urine and prescribe antibiotics.

Complementary therapies

Complementary therapies are sometimes used by parents looking for ways of soothing their babies' crying. Massage is used to boost a baby's well-being and promote relaxation and bonding (see pages 40–41), while homeopathy can help with digestive problems.

Before visiting any complementary practitioner, you should ensure that he or she is registered and specializes in working with babies and children.

Questions & Answers

Whenever my baby cries more than usual, I always worry that he may be sick. My biggest fear is meningitis. How will I know?
This is a rare and extremely serious illness, but babies can recover with antibiotics if it is caught early. So if you ever suspect it, **take your baby to the hospital immediately**. There are viral and bacterial types, and signs to look out for are a high-pitched, moaning cry, a very high temperature, the appearance of sleepiness, and the refusal to eat. One type, meningococcal meningitis, produces a red or purplish rash that doesn't fade when pressed with the side of a clear glass or your finger. Other types do not produce a rash, so never wait for this sign—seek medical help **as soon as possible**. There are vaccinations for meningitis C and *Haemophilus influenzae* type b (Hib).

" I love to watch my baby when he's asleep. Sometimes he lies **still and peaceful**, and other times he **wriggles and twitches**. He even smiles as though he's having a lovely dream. "

EVA, mother of three-week-old Jake

The importance of sleep in the first months

Sleep is a precious commodity, both for your baby and for you. And it's not just the quantity of sleep that's important—it's the quality, too. Sleep affects every aspect of our lives, and understanding what happens when we sleep is the first step toward helping your baby develop healthy sleeping habits that will benefit the whole family.

Sleep stages

Your baby's days are divided into periods of sleep and wakefulness. His sleep periods consist of two distinct states, which are very similar to the sleep stages all of us experience:

● **Active sleep (so called in newborn babies), also known as rapid-eye-movement (REM) sleep** Although the full function of REM sleep remains a mystery, it is known to be essential to the development and maintenance of the brain.

Newborn babies spend around half their sleep time in REM sleep, while in adulthood, REM sleep accounts only for approximately 20 percent of our sleep.

● **Quiet sleep (newborns) or non-REM sleep** Here, your baby's sleep is more peaceful and his brain is less active. Non-REM sleep consists of four phases of gradually deepening sleep: drowsiness, light sleep, deep sleep, and very deep sleep. Your baby will go through these phases in "cycles," alternating periods of REM and non-REM sleep. During the progression into deepest sleep, your baby is less active and his breathing slows.

Unlike during REM sleep, very little, if any, dreaming occurs in this stage.

Sleep cycles

Your newborn sleeps in cycles of around 50 or 60 minutes of alternating REM and non-REM sleep. These cycles become longer as he matures. Like you, your baby wakes up several

REM AND NON-REM SLEEP
Your newborn spends around half the time that he's asleep in REM sleep (left). During this stage, his eyes flick beneath his eyelids, or he may twitch his fingers and toes. The rest of the time, he's in deep, non-REM sleep (right), when he's very quiet and still.

Questions & Answers

Do premature babies have different sleep patterns?

Yes. Premature babies tend to wake more often at night than full-term infants for the first few months, and possibly for up to a year. Night-waking and lighter sleep are part of a premature baby's built-in survival mechanism—he's able to wake up easily so that he can be fed. He will sleep much more than a full-term baby, and a larger proportion of his sleep time (up to 90 percent) will be spent in REM sleep. His sleep patterns will settle down in time, but they will take longer than those of a full-term baby.

Does my baby dream?

It is not known for sure whether babies dream, but it seems very likely. Dreams take place during REM sleep, and babies spend a large part of their sleep time in this stage. Experts are not entirely sure why we dream. Some believe that it helps the brain to process information and exercise the synapses, or pathways, between brain cells. Interestingly, our brain waves during dream sleep, as recorded by machines, are almost identical in nature to the brain waves during the hours we spend awake. This is not the case during the other phases of sleep.

times in the night as part of his natural sleep cycle. If he is able to lull himself back to sleep, this stirring will pass unnoticed. If he can't go back to sleep without help from you, he may become fully awake and cry. This is a common reason for disturbed nights, and one that can be solved by teaching your baby how to soothe himself back to sleep.

How many hours?

Parents commonly ask how much sleep their baby needs. The answer is not straightforward, because every baby's sleep needs are different. Newborns have no regular pattern and may sleep from as little as 10½ hours to 20 hours out of 24. From two to three months, nighttime sleep averages about nine hours, in addition to about five hours of naps throughout the day. By 12 months, your baby's nighttime sleep will be around 11½ hours, with 2½ hours of daytime naps.

Evolving patterns

At around 8 to 12 weeks, you may notice your baby's sleep becoming more regular, and you will be able to start guiding him into a day–night sleep routine. He may naturally begin to show a preference for nighttime sleeping at this stage, and he'll probably spend longer periods awake and active during the day.

Healthy habits

Although your baby doesn't need to be taught how to sleep, healthy sleep habits are something he will have to learn. Whether he sleeps soundly or not depends to a great extent on what you teach him. This is not as daunting as it may sound, and the sooner you start, the easier it will be.

● **Establish a routine** Babies, toddlers, and children are comforted by familiarity (see page 72). Regular bedtime habits will help your baby understand that soon it will be time to go to sleep.

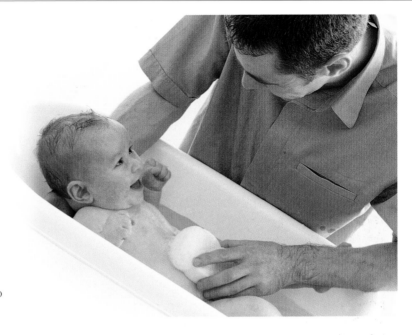

● **Teach your baby to fall asleep by himself** This is one of the most valuable lessons you can teach your baby. Many experts believe that, after the newborn phase, putting your baby to bed by rocking him or feeding him prevents him from developing self-soothing behaviors. Instead, they recommend putting your baby to bed when he's still awake, well-fed, sleepy, and able to fall asleep without help from you.

● **Make sure he gets daytime rest** While it is a good idea to limit the length of daytime naps to maintain a contrast between night and day, keeping your baby awake when he wants to sleep makes him overtired. He will find it harder to settle down and sleep soundly.

A RELAXING BATH
Many babies find a warm bath relaxing, which makes it a perfect way to end the day as part of a bedtime routine.

● **Be aware of your baby's needs** Respond quickly to a sudden change in your baby's sleep pattern. If he is teething or has a cold, you may need to alter his bedtime and naptime routines for a while. A baby who is ill needs plenty of cuddles and extra care. Once he's well again, return to your established routine.

● **Be consistent** Changing your baby's daytime routines and allowing him to sleep in different places, rather than just in his crib, is fine once in a while, but if it happens too often, it can become a habit and lead to problems.

Expert tips

Crib safety

• Make sure your baby's crib is safety-approved. All modern crib designs are required by law to meet certain standards.

• Crib bars should be no more than 2³/₈in (6cm) apart, to avoid your baby's head and limbs getting stuck.

• Most cribs have an adjustable mattress level. Start by using the highest level for easy access in the first months and finish on the lowest level once your baby is able to sit up. There must be at least 26in (66cm) between the mattress support and the crib sides in the raised position. When the crib side is lowered, there should be a distance of at least 9in (23cm).

• There should be no horizontal bars, which may allow your baby to climb up and possibly fall out.

• Every time you put your baby in her crib, check that the drop-side mechanism is locked. Never leave your baby in her crib with the side down.

The mattress

• The crib mattress should fit tightly. If you can slide two fingers between the crib sides or ends and the mattress, the mattress is too small.

• Mattresses are made of foam or natural fibers. Either is fine, as long as the mattress is firm and fits snugly.

• Keep your baby's mattress well-aired and clean. Mattresses with a vinyl surface or a removable washable cover are easiest to clean.

Where should she sleep?

New babies are better off sleeping near their parents during the early weeks. You might prefer to start by having your baby in a bassinet beside your bed, and then move her into her own room when she is more settled. Bassinets are cozy and practical. A good one should be firm but snug for your baby. They usually come with a valance that makes a frill around the outside, a liner, and a mattress. Make sure the mattress fits snugly (see "Expert Tips," left). Once your baby begins to roll, or simply grows too long for the bassinet, it's time to move her to a crib.

Cradles

You may choose to use a cradle in the early months instead of a

A BASSINET

A bassinet is the ideal size for your new baby, and can be carried from room to room if necessary—although never when your baby is inside it!

bassinet. Cradles have many of the advantages of bassinets, but they are not portable. The main difference is that they can be rocked, and your newborn may find this very soothing. If you choose a rocking cradle, make sure you can lock it in a stationary position while your baby is sleeping, and that it cannot be tipped over.

Choosing a crib

Your baby can sleep in a crib from the start, but you may prefer to wait until she is past the newborn stage before you transfer her from her bassinet or cradle.

You can expect your baby to sleep in a crib until she's at least 18 months old, and possibly up to three years. You will know when she has outgrown it because she'll start trying to climb out of it!

There are several points to consider when choosing a crib:

● **Sturdiness** Once your baby is able to sit up and move around, a sturdy crib is a must.

● **Drop sides** One or both of the crib sides should drop for easy access. The catch mechanism needs to be very sturdy, because you will soon have a baby who can jump up and down and rattle the bars. Look for a drop mechanism that you can

DROP SIDES
The drop-side mechanism on your baby's crib should be easy to operate, preferably with one hand, yet secure. Never leave the side down when your baby is in the crib.

open with one hand, if possible.

● **Teething rails** Once she can stand, your baby may want to try out her new teeth on the top of her crib. Most cribs have rigid plastic strips along the top rails to protect

her from splinters and the crib from being damaged.

● **Casters** Some cribs are sold with casters, which make them easier to move around for cleaning. Ensure that the casters can be locked.

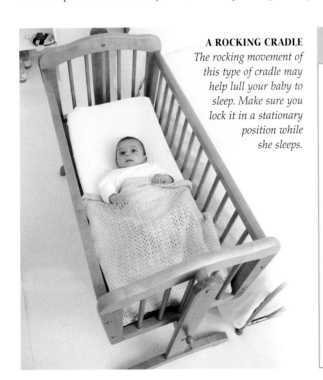

A ROCKING CRADLE
The rocking movement of this type of cradle may help lull your baby to sleep. Make sure you lock it in a stationary position while she sleeps.

Multipurpose designs

Instead of a conventional crib, you may decide to choose a crib that is designed to meet specific needs.

● **A bedside crib** has a removable side so that it can become an extension of your bed at night. This is becoming an increasingly popular way of sleeping with your baby.

● **A rocking cradle** can be rocked, which many babies will find soothing, or it can be locked into static mode.

● **A crib-bed** can be used as a crib in the early years and then, by removing the sides, can be transformed into a small bed when your child is old enough. It is a good idea, but a crib-bed is usually more expensive than a normal crib, and you will at some stage need to buy a full-size bed for your child. Also, as your family grows, you might need the crib again for another baby while your older child is still using it as a bed.

How can I keep my baby safe?

Although it is rare, all parents worry about the possibility of Sudden Infant Death Syndrome (SIDS), the leading cause of death in babies between one month and one year of age. The causes of this tragic syndrome are not yet fully understood, but there are some important precautions you can take to reduce the risk significantly.

The following recommendations apply throughout your baby's first year, although they are particularly important during the first six months, when the incidence of SIDS is at its highest. If your baby sleeps with a babysitter or other caregiver, make sure they also follow these guidelines.

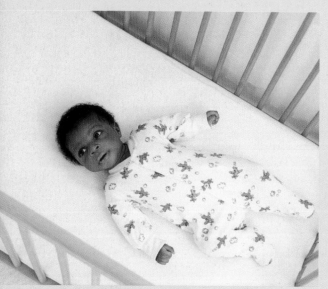

FEET TO FOOT
Always place your baby with her feet to the foot of the crib, cradle, or bassinet. This safety measure ensures that she cannot slip under or become entangled with her bedclothes, if you are using them, and allows her to wriggle free of her covers if she becomes too hot.

★ **Always put your baby down to sleep on her back** Studies have proven that putting your baby to sleep on her back significantly lowers the risk of SIDS. Once your baby is older, she will be able to turn herself onto her stomach. However, you should continue to put her to sleep on her back even if she does change position during the night.

★ **Never smoke around your baby** You should also keep her away from smoky atmospheres. Babies who are exposed to cigarette smoke are at a higher risk of dying from SIDS.

★ **Keep your baby's bedroom at the right temperature** A room temperature of around 65°F (18°C) is ideal. Overheating can be life-threatening because your baby cannot yet regulate her own temperature properly. The best way to test if she is becoming too hot is to feel her bare tummy or the nape of her neck.

★ **Place her with her feet at the foot of the crib, bassinet, or cradle** This is vital, because it stops your baby from slipping under the covers and suffocating. You should always keep her head uncovered.

★ **Never use comforters, quilts, or thick blankets** Soft bedding can cause your baby to overheat. It is best to use a sheet, or one or two layers of thin blankets, that are securely tucked into the sides and foot of the mattress, no higher than your baby's chest. In warmer weather, take off a layer or remove bedcovers altogether.

★ **Never use crib bumpers or a pillow** These can contribute to overheating, and can also suffocate your baby. For similar reasons, you should never leave soft toys in her crib or put your baby to sleep on top of a cushion, beanbag, or waterbed. Also, avoid falling asleep with your baby on a sofa.

★ **Never use hot-water bottles** You should also never use electric blankets in your baby's bed.

★ **Use a firm mattress, and clean and air it regularly** Also make sure that there is no gap between the edges and the sides of the crib (see page 54).

★ **Seek medical advice promptly** if your baby is sick.

YOUR BABY'S BEDDING
If you use bedding, use a sheet or one or two thin blankets that reach no higher than your baby's chest, securely tucked in on all sides.

> *" Nathan feeds greedily at first, followed by little bursts of comfort sucks, before falling happily asleep. "*

MARTHA, mother of five-week-old Nathan

Your baby's movements

While sleeping, your baby may:

● be very busy twitching, jerking, sucking, snuffling, or smiling. This is normal. Even with all this activity, he is actually getting a sound sleep. These movements happen when your baby is in REM, or "dream," sleep (see page 51)

● suddenly "jump" in his sleep occasionally. This is due to a normal reflex called the "startle" or Moro reflex. It sometimes occurs for no apparent reason, although often it is a response to a loud noise or sudden jolt. It may seem troubling to you, but the reflex is actually a reassuring sign that your baby's neurological system is functioning well. It will disappear by around four months.

The first few weeks

Wakefulness for the first few hours after birth, followed by a long stretch of up to 24 hours of very sound sleep, is a normal pattern for newborns. At this stage, he will probably be alert only for short periods every day; he's not mature enough to benefit from longer periods of alertness, and sleep (particularly REM sleep) helps him to mature.

Gradually, these periods of wakefulness will grow longer, so that by the end of the first month he may be awake for a total of two or three hours during the day, most of it in one long stretch. He may also begin to sleep for longer periods, so that instead of one or two hours, he may be able to sleep for three or four.

Sleeping and feeding

It's natural for a newborn to fall asleep while nursing or sucking on a bottle. After the first few weeks, you may want to change this habit so that you put him down while he's still awake but drowsy.

A newborn may take most of his feeding during the first five minutes or so, and once he's full, he may doze off contentedly at the breast or bottle. But if he hasn't emptied your breast or the bottle, gently wake him up after a few minutes and offer him some more. If he's still hungry, he'll finish his feeding.

Healthcare providers recommend that newborn babies should not sleep longer than three or four hours without feeding. At this stage, your baby needs constant nourishment and should be woken up. If he doesn't wake up when you pick him up, try sitting him on your lap and gently bending him forward. When he stirs, put him in position for feeding, with your nipple or the bottle's nipple close to his lips. Try changing his diaper, tickling his feet, or brushing his cheek with either your nipple or the bottle's. If all attempts fail, leave him a little longer and then try again. But never let him go more than five hours without a feeding.

Sleeping and crying

Your baby cries because it is the only way he can communicate—it's his way of telling you he's hungry, in pain, in need of a cuddle, or simply sleepy. At first, it's hard to interpret your baby's different cries, but as you get to know him, you'll respond to them more easily.

Using a pacifier

To ensure that the pacifier does not become a habit, you should plan to use it only during the early months, and try to restrict it to bedtime only. A pacifier can soothe your baby to sleep and, if he keeps hold of it, he may be less likely to wake up after a disturbance or during the lighter stages of his sleep cycle. However, pacifiers often fall out during sleep, disturbing your baby. He may start crying until you come and find it again. Pacifiers can limit sound-making, and may stop him from exploring toys with his mouth later.

Questions & Answers

Should I let my newborn baby cry?

Letting your baby "cry it out" is not advisable, particularly for the first few weeks of life. At this early stage, your baby needs you to respond to his needs promptly. You cannot "spoil" him by giving him attention; in fact, the more attention he gets, the more you reassure him that he is valued and that his needs are important. In a few months, when you get to know your baby, you may decide to let him cry for certain short periods at a time—for example, if you are "sleep training" and you know that he isn't crying out of pain, hunger, or discomfort. But during the first few weeks, your baby will not benefit from this technique.

Inconsolable and excessive crying

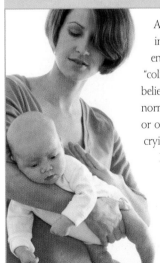

A baby who cries regularly and inconsolably for long periods, usually at the end of the day, is often described as having "colic" (see pages 42–43), which experts now believe may be simply an extreme form of normal crying. Your baby could be overtired or overstimulated, and once he's started crying, he doesn't know how to stop.

It can be upsetting to see your baby in distress and not be able to soothe him,

A SOOTHING HOLD
Lay your baby across your forearm and, keeping a steadying grasp between his legs, gently rub or pat his back.

but colic is not serious and it does no long-term damage. By three or four months, it will have stopped. A baby with colic may cry himself to sleep, but stay with him, preferably in a darkened, quiet room. You can also try:

● doing a "colic dance," rocking him up and down while swaying your hips

● gently rubbing his abdomen, or patting his back while holding him across your forearm or up against your shoulder

● giving him a bath, but stop if he becomes more agitated

● giving him a massage (see pages 40–41).

How can I help my newborn sleep?

Sometimes your new baby will fall asleep at the drop of a hat, but there will be other occasions when he refuses to settle down, waking up and crying every time you put him down. Keep in mind that he's only recently left the warm, cozy, and secure environment of your womb—it can take some time to adapt to his strange new world. The key to coping in the early days is to help him feel comfortable and secure, creating a soothing environment for him.

USE A CARRIER
The more you can hold your new baby close, the more secure and settled he'll be. A carrier helps you hold him while keeping both hands free.

Ways to soothe your newborn

★ **Calming movement** When he was in the womb, your baby was lulled by the motion of you going about your daily business. Out of the womb, movement still has this effect on him. Rocking, swaying, and patting while he's cuddled up in your arms will all contribute to contentment—and sleep—during these early weeks. After a few months, it is best to help your baby learn to self-soothe and fall asleep on his own. But for now, he needs you.

★ **Gentle sound** In the womb, your baby was used to hearing the comforting sounds of your heartbeat, the gurgling of your stomach, and the soft tones of your voice. Now that he's born, sleeping may be difficult without some background noise. He might like you talking quietly, singing, or humming to him. Or he may be soothed by the rhythmic hum of a fan or the washing machine, or strains of music from a radio. You could even play him a recording of womb sounds.

★ **Helping him feel secure** Because your baby is used to being curled up in a tight space, the vast expanse of a crib may make him feel insecure. If your baby seems uncomfortable in a crib, then a cradle or a bassinet can be used to provide a snug fit that's closer to the nine-month-long embrace in the womb. For added security, try swaddling (see page 37).

★ **A full tummy** If possible, make the last feeding you give your baby before bedtime a full one. If he nods off before he has had enough, change his position, tickle his toes, and rouse him so that he can finish feeding. Otherwise, you may find he will soon wake up again for his second course.

★ **Soothing smells** Your baby has a very good sense of smell and, in particular, he will find your individual scent very comforting. So, you could try stuffing a muslin square or a handkerchief into your shirt for a short while so that it smells like you and then placing it safely in his crib, bassinet, or cradle.

SING TO HIM
He loves the sound of your voice, and he's trying hard to focus on your face. Try singing to him, and gently swaying your hips from side to side as you cradle him in your arms.

GO FOR A WALK
The fresh air and the sights and sounds of the great outdoors will soon tire your baby. He'll also be soothed by the steady movement of the stroller.

A GOOD FEEDING
Your baby will settle down nicely if he's feeling full. If he empties one breast and still seems hungry, offer him the other one. Try burping him before putting him down.

3-6
months

"She's now beginning to take a **real interest** in her toys, which is fascinating to watch."

ROGER, father of four-month-old Keira

" Expressing my breast milk means that I have a little more **freedom** and time **for myself** while Tim feeds Matthew. "

JULIA, mother of four-month-old Matthew

Expressing breast milk

By the third month you will probably be feeling more confident about breastfeeding your baby: feeding should be settling into a pattern, and any early problems that you may have encountered will hopefully have been resolved. You may also be thinking about expressing milk for your baby at around this time.

What is expressing?

Sometimes babies and their mothers can't be together all the time. Fortunately, direct mother-to-baby feeding isn't the only way to give your baby breast milk: If you have to spend some or all of the day away from her, expressing milk provides you with an alternative method.

Expressing means squeezing the milk out of your breasts. It's done either by hand, or using an electric or manual pump. The milk is then stored in bottles or bags in the refrigerator or freezer to be used whenever your baby needs to be fed and you can't do it directly. There are a number of reasons why some babies and their mothers can't be together. For example, in some instances a baby may need to stay in a neonatal intensive care unit (NICU) if she was born prematurely, or if she has a medical condition that requires immediate treatment.

Another reason for expressing might be if the mother chooses or feels she has no choice but to go back to work outside the home, and is unable to have her baby cared for on or close to her employer's premises. In either of these cases, being able to express milk, which is then fed to the baby when the mother isn't around, makes the difference between having to stop breastfeeding and being able to continue.

A third category of mothers who might want to learn to express are those who have occasional reason to be apart from their babies—the occasional day away or overnight trip when they leave their babies with others.

Expressing milk if your baby needs special care

This is the hardest situation in which to express because, unlike a mother who's returning to work, and who's already an experienced breastfeeder, you'll be starting your life as a breastfeeding mother with only a pump to get the milk to flow. Emotionally, you may be in a difficult situation—your pregnancy might have ended in an entirely unexpected way, and now you find yourself with a tiny baby who may need to stay in the hospital for a long time, and who you'd desperately like to breastfeed. For the next few weeks, the time you spend

Expert tip

Hand expression (see page 66) is a useful skill for any breastfeeding mother to master. For example, you can relieve the pressure of engorged breasts by expressing some milk gently while sitting in a warm bath. And rubbing a little expressed milk onto a sore or cracked nipple can help it to heal.

How do I express?

Expressing techniques depend on whether you're using a pump or expressing by hand. Remember that practice is hugely important—this is an entirely learned skill, and the more you do it, the more efficient and confident you will become. Some women find that taking a warm shower or bath before they start can encourage the milk to flow.

will start to drip from your breasts. At the first few pumping sessions, you're unlikely to come away with more than a few drops. But over time, your efforts will result in a lot more milk being collected.

Expressing by hand

Hand expressing is a useful skill. Wash your hands before you start. Then place your thumbs above your nipple and your fingers below so they form a circle around your areola. Squeeze gently, pushing the glands behind the areola in a circular motion. Use a sterile bowl to collect the milk. Hand expressing is time-consuming at first, but some women go on to be experts and find it almost as efficient as a pump.

Expressing with a pump

Whether you're using an electric, battery-operated, or manual pump, you'll start by holding the cup and bottle attachment to your nipple, ensuring that as much of the areola as possible is covered by the cup.

Switch the machine on or, if you are using a hand pump, start to activate the suction process with the handle. The suction mimics the way a baby sucks at the nipple, drawing it out rhythmically, and milk

SPECIAL-CARE BABIES
*Expressing milk to feed to your special-care baby helps reassure you
that you are giving your baby the very best nourishment.*

pumping milk may be frustrating because every part of you yearns to be cuddling your tiny baby and feeding her skin-to-skin. But the breast pump can be your friend, too, because without the stimulation it provides, it's extremely difficult to keep your milk supply going in order to feed the baby herself when she's bigger.

Premature babies either can't suck or can't suck very efficiently— they're just too little, born before the sucking reflex has been properly developed. The milk you express can only be fed into your baby's tiny body by tube—you'll probably be able to assist in this by holding the tube during the feeding. Because your breasts are being stimulated only via the pump, you need to express milk regularly and often. Keeping your supply going will be one of the biggest challenges. Some things to try include:

• getting a special "dual-cup" attachment for the breast pump you use, so that you can express milk from both breasts at the same time— this helps increase your milk production by making your body think you're feeding two babies

• waking at night to express—this increases your supply because your levels of prolactin, which switches on the milk-producing cells in your breasts, are higher at night

• looking at a picture of your baby as you're expressing, which can encourage your milk to let down.

Which kind of breast pump?

• **Hospital–grade electric pumps**
Best for mothers whose babies are in the hospital, these pumps, which are expensive and therefore usually available for rent, are the best substitute for a baby's mouth in efficiently removing milk from the breast. If your baby is in a special- care unit and is too small or too weak to suck directly from your breasts, this kind of pump will keep your milk supply going until your baby is old enough and strong enough to do it herself.

• **AC–powered portable pumps**
Portable electric pumps provide a means for expressing at home for a mother who's spending much of her time in the hospital with her baby. They're also useful for working mothers who need to express often.

• **Battery-operated pumps**
These are not as strong as either of the above pumps, but they are light and easy to carry and a useful backup for a working mother who needs to travel away from her office on occasion.

• **Hand-operated pumps**
These work by squeezing a handle to produce a vacuum in a cup attached to your nipple, encouraging the milk to flow. They are more time-consuming than other pumps, and also harder work, but are useful for mothers who want to express only occasionally, or who want to try it without a big financial outlay.

How can I store my milk?

You'll need to put your expressed milk in special plastic bottles or in plastic bags made for the purpose. Remember to write the date on the bag. To make sure milk is stored in sterilized containers, you can boil them for 10 minutes or put them in the dishwasher. If you are using bottles to feed your baby expressed milk, these will have to be carefully cleaned and sterilized since milk can harbor germs.

Fresh breast milk stored in the refrigerator should be used within 24 hours. Frozen milk lasts up to three months, and up to 24 hours once defrosted. However, freezing destroys some of the antibodies in milk, so use fresh milk whenever possible. But even thawed milk is better than formula in terms of its health-giving properties. Put the bottle or bag of frozen milk into

MILK STORAGE
You can store your milk in special plastic bags or bottles.

a bowl of warm water to thaw, or defrost it in the refrigerator overnight. Don't put expressed milk in the microwave, because this will kill some of the nutrients. And even though you might be tempted not to, always throw away any remaining expressed milk at the end of a feeding—don't keep it for a later feeding because it may harbor germs.

Expressing if you are going back to work

Expressing is a good option if you're returning to work while your baby is still relatively young—maybe only three or four months old—and is still exclusively breastfed. After about six months, when your baby is starting to eat solid foods, you may want to adjust your feeding schedule and increase the number of feedings she has when you're together, and let her get by with formula from a cup or bottle when you're at work.

Planning to express

Expressing is time-consuming and can be a complicated procedure to set up at work, but it does ensure that your baby can have as much breast milk as she needs, even when

Questions & Answers

I'm going back to work in eight weeks. Should I start to express?
Start getting used to expressing and build up a good freezer supply of milk a few weeks before you go back to work. Knowing you are adept at expressing will make you a lot more confident about your return. Also, knowing there are plenty of bottles of milk in the freezer will take the pressure off you to produce lots of milk once you are back at work.

My baby will be in a special-care unit for at least a month. How often should I express?
The answer to this depends on your individual ability to produce milk—some women need more breast stimulation than others to do this successfully. As a rough guide, you will probably need to express between six and eight times in 24 hours. Consider expressing at night if your milk production seems to be going down, since this will give it a boost.

How long should each session of expressing with an electric breast pump take?
As time goes on you will become increasingly efficient at expressing, but you probably need to spend at least 30 minutes at a time with the pump. It's worth stopping and starting, and switching sides, for maximum effect. When you first start using a pump, the trick is to go for frequent short sessions.

you're not able to be physically with her for a feeding.

Becoming a working mother who expresses takes some organization. Start while you're still pregnant by preparing the ground at your workplace for the expressing sessions you'll need to start once you go back.

Talk to your manager, and explain that while you're committed to your job, you're also committed to breastfeeding. Tell your supervisor that many other women have managed to achieve what you're hoping for, and reassure her that it won't affect your ability to do your job. In fact, many women who express at work say they find it easier to concentrate on their job because they know that although they can't be with their children, they're doing their very best for them.

How will it work?

It's best to think very carefully about where you will express at work, and where you will store your milk, before you talk to your supervisor. Unless you're in the fortunate position of having other women in your workplace regularly express, it may be a new issue for your managers, and it's best if you go prepared with the answers to the questions they are likely to ask.

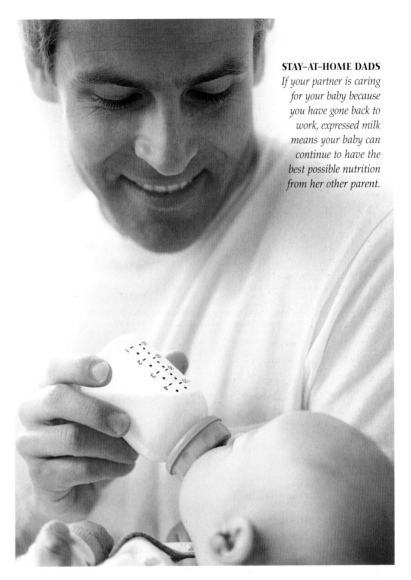

STAY-AT-HOME DADS
If your partner is caring for your baby because you have gone back to work, expressed milk means your baby can continue to have the best possible nutrition from her other parent.

These will probably include:
● Where will you express your breast milk? You will need a reasonably comfortable space where you can be assured privacy.
● Where will you store the milk? You'll need a refrigerator—you might want to consider investing in your own personal mini-fridge to help you keep your milk out of view of your colleagues.
● Will your breast pump remain on the premises during nights and weekends, and if so, will it be insured?
● How much time is expressing milk going to take out of your workday?

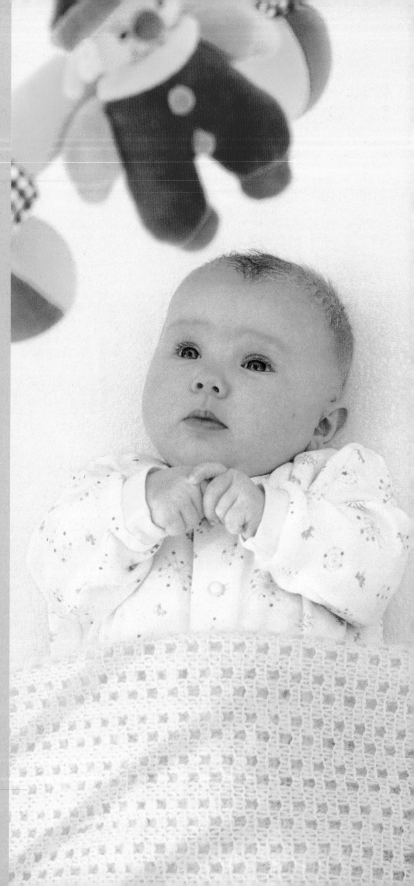

" We've hung a brightly colored **musical mobile** over Susannah's crib. I always turn it on as I say good night, and she usually falls asleep listening to its gentle **lullaby. "**

JAN, mother of four-month-old Susannah

Encouraging good sleep habits

At around two to three months, you may see a change in your baby's sleeping patterns. She will probably have more periods during the day when she's showing an interest in her surroundings. At night, she may be sleeping for longer stretches. This is the ideal time to start encouraging her to adopt good sleeping habits.

Changing patterns

By now, your baby will be alert for longer periods during the day, and she may also be starting to sleep for longer stretches at night. A rhythm to her sleeping and waking times will soon emerge, and over the coming weeks, you will probably see these patterns taking a definite shape.

At six months old, most babies' sleep is consolidated into one longer sleep at night and several shorter sleeps during the day. There are a number of factors that contribute to these changes in your baby's sleeping patterns:

● Her sleep–wake cycles are becoming less dependent on hunger. As her stomach capacity grows, she can go longer without needing to feed. She may even drop one of her night feedings. By six months, when solid foods account for a substantial part of her diet, most—but not all—babies will sleep for a six-hour stretch without waking.

● Your baby's internal body clock is beginning to tick. This means that she will spend more time awake during the day and more time asleep at night. Her body clock is regulated by internal factors like hunger and tiredness, as well as external ones, such as light and dark, and her day-to-day schedule.

● Her mental and social skills are developing so that she is able to recognize and respond to your cues. For example, if you give her a bath before bedtime every night, she will now have the capacity to remember that after a bath, it's time for her to settle down and go to sleep.

Expert tips

Between two and six months, your baby will start to give you cues that she is getting sleepy and is ready for a nap or bedtime. She may:

● decrease her level of activity and become quiet

● lose interest in people or toys

● start yawning

● rub her eyes

● look "glazed"

● become fussy or irritable

● bury her head in your chest or turn away from you.

Checklist

Your baby's bedtime routine can include any (or all) of the following activities:

- giving her a bath
- giving her a gentle massage
- putting on her sleeper
- reading a bedtime story
- singing to her
- cuddling her
- feeding her
- kissing her good night.

Helping your baby sleep

From around three months, you can help teach your baby to adopt healthy sleep patterns by doing two very important things:

- gently teaching her how to go to sleep by herself
- establishing a bedtime routine.

At some point, you will want your baby to feel secure enough to go to sleep and stay asleep without needing you there (see below). If she is able to do this, she will sleep better, which will have a positive impact on her physical and mental development. It also means that you and your whole family will reap the rewards—eventually—by having fewer disturbed nights.

Starting a routine

When your baby was a newborn, deciding when to put her down for the night was as easy as watching for the signs of sleepiness she gave, such as crying, yawning, or rubbing her eyes.

While your baby may still do these things (and you should still respond to them), you don't need to wait for

Steps to a good night's sleep

1 For your baby to learn how to sleep by herself, she needs to be put to bed while she is still awake. Instead of rocking her to sleep or allowing her to doze off while feeding, keep her awake: Sing or talk to her in a soft voice, stroke her head, or cuddle her.

2 When she is drowsy, put her into her crib on her back. At first, she may become more awake and fuss or cry. Soothe her gently, say good night in a soft voice, and leave.

3 If she cries, resist going back for a few minutes. If she carries on, go in to her, stroke her, but don't pick her up.

4 When she is calm, leave the room again. If she continues to cry, wait a little longer than last time, then repeat the soothing visit. You may have to do this many times, but if you are consistent, within a few nights she will be going to sleep by herself. Some babies go to sleep with the help of a soothing sensation, such as sucking a thumb or pacifier (see page 59). Others prefer the feel of a soft toy or blanket. Never put your baby to bed with a bottle—this can cause tooth decay.

5 If your baby wakes during the night, and she is not due for a feeding or crying out of pain or discomfort, repeat these steps, waiting for a few minutes before soothing her and leaving the room again.

Questions & Answers

Should I let my baby fall asleep at the breast?
It's natural for a baby to fall asleep while sucking at the breast or on a bottle. While it's fine to let your newborn do this, if it becomes a habit, over time she will learn to associate sucking with falling asleep, and may eventually not be able to fall asleep in any other way. If you want your baby to be able to go to sleep without your help, remove the breast or bottle when she appears to be dropping off. At first, your baby may resist and start to fuss and try to find the nipple or bottle again. Let her do this, but as she starts to fall asleep again, remove the nipple or bottle again. You may need to repeat this many times, but eventually, your baby will learn to fall asleep without a nipple or bottle in her mouth.

these signs before you put her to bed. You can now take more control of bedtimes, by putting her down at roughly the same time every night, with a similar routine.

At first, this will be a bit hit-and-miss because her feeding and napping habits can still be unpredictable. But introducing a routine now can go a long way toward regulating these patterns and setting her body clock to a healthy schedule.

She will probably respond well to routine at this stage, and enjoy the rituals of getting ready for her nighttime sleep.

The following tips will help you establish a bedtime routine that works for both you and your baby.

● **Choose your baby's bedtime** Try to stick to it as much as possible. Normally, her bedtime should be any time between 7:00 pm and 8:30 pm. If you put her to bed any later than 8:30 pm, there is a risk that she may become overtired.

● **Be consistent** Try to follow the same sequence of events at around the same time every evening.

● **Always keep your routine manageable** Elaborate routines can become drawn out indefinitely, which means that you will be spending longer than necessary settling your baby to sleep and thus defeating the object of the exercise.

● **Try to stick to a daytime routine, too** Your baby will now have longer periods of wakefulness during the day, so you will have the opportunity to give the day more of a structure. Having regular times for playing, feeding, and napping, for example, can be beneficial for you and your baby.

● **Be flexible** Having a routine doesn't mean you have to stick to it rigidly. It will vary sometimes, depending on what you're doing during the day and how tired your baby is. Be consistent, but know when to bend the rules.

How can I help my baby settle down at night—and sleep through?

A bedtime routine helps your baby recognize that it's time to go to sleep—and the ideal time to start a simple routine is at around the age of three months. Once she is settled, there are steps you can take to ensure that she doesn't wake up unnecessarily.

Starting a routine

Think carefully about what you would like to include in your young baby's bedtime routine, because whatever you establish now may later become a habit that will be hard to break. You can always add to her routine as she gets older (see pages 116–117) but, for now, keep it simple. Your aim should be to create a peaceful, relaxing end to her increasingly busy day. Try the following:

★ **A warm bath** As well as a practical way of keeping her clean, a gentle splash in the water before bed can be enjoyable.

★ **A massage** Massage is known to boost a baby's feeling of well-being, and is a perfect way to help her relax before bed, especially after her bath.

★ **A cuddle and a feeding** Once she's dressed, a cuddle and a good feeding will help her go to bed contentedly. Try to ensure that you put her down when she is awake but drowsy.

A BATH
A bath can help your baby wind down. Make sure the bathroom is warm and have a towel, a fresh diaper, and her sleeper at hand. Wrap her up and give her a big hug!

Why is she waking up?

Erratic sleep patterns are normal during the early months, but you can start to help your baby sleep through the night by considering why she's waking up and trying to eliminate the cause.

★ **Is she hungry?** If she suddenly starts waking up more frequently, she may be having a growth spurt, which means she needs more milk to be sustained.

★ **Is she uncomfortable?** Always check that your baby is not in pain, that her diaper is not wet or soiled, and that she's not too hot or cold (see pages 56–57). Check for a fever or other signs of illness. If you suspect she is ill, call your healthcare provider.

★ **Is she being disturbed?** If she sleeps in your room, she may hear you stirring, so think about moving her to her own room.

★ **Is her room too dark or too light?** Your baby needs just enough light to reassure her that she's in familiar surroundings. A simple night-light can solve this problem. Room-darkening shades will help block out unwanted light.

★ **Are you sure she's really awake?** Sometimes, you may think your baby is waking up when she's just in a phase of light sleep. Or she may be awake but about to drift back to sleep if not stimulated. When you know she's not ill or hungry, let her fuss for a few minutes before going to her.

★ **Can she fall asleep by herself?** Putting her down while drowsy but still awake will help her learn to fall asleep by herself (see page 72).

A MASSAGE
Massage your baby using light, circular or sweeping strokes all over her body, and a little baby oil if you wish. As you massage her, talk softly to her and maintain eye contact.

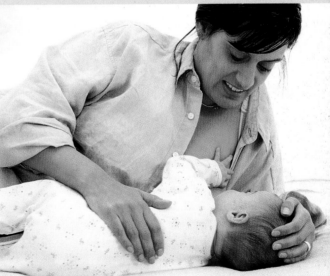

A CUDDLE AND A FEEDING
Make sure that the last feeding your baby has before bedtime is a full feeding, so she doesn't wake up too soon feeling hungry. If she falls asleep before she is finished, try to rouse her.

Coping with early risers

If your baby regularly wakes up too early in the morning, you can sometimes solve the problem by putting room-darkening curtains or blinds on the window in her room to block out the morning light. Don't go to her right away when she wakes up and fusses—leave her for a little while to see if she will go back to sleep.

Some healthcare providers recommend helping your baby "readjust" her body clock by keeping her up an extra hour at night, but there is no guarantee that this will work. If you do try it, it's worth persisting for several nights to see if there is a difference in her waking time, because changes won't take effect immediately.

Unfortunately, many babies and children are simply unable to sleep late in the morning and wake up just because they have had enough sleep. You may have to adapt to her pattern for a while. At around six months, you can put some of her favorite toys in her crib to keep her occupied while you catch a few more precious minutes of sleep.

Questions & Answers

How do I know whether my baby is getting enough sleep?
Many babies regulate themselves pretty well when it comes to getting their quota of sleep, but not every baby gets as much as she needs. If she is frequently irritable and hard to please, it may be that your baby isn't napping enough or getting enough total sleep. If you believe your baby needs more sleep, try putting her down earlier, even if she cries for a while, and leaving her for a few minutes if she wakes in the night or too early in the morning, to see if she goes back to sleep. But if she sleeps less than the "average" for her age and seems happy, then she's probably getting enough sleep and just happens not to need as much as other babies.

LONGER NAPS
It's better for your baby to have longer naps of good quality sleep than to snatch several short naps during the day.

Daytime naps

The length and quality of your baby's daytime naps will affect her nighttime sleep—and vice versa. By four or five months, the typical baby takes three or four regular naps of an hour or so each during the day. Some babies will take two longer ones of around 90 minutes or more.

Longer naps may be more beneficial for your baby. Catnapping during the day—falling asleep in sporadic bursts of half an hour or so—does not have the same effect, and your baby may follow the same pattern during the night, waking up frequently. So try to encourage your baby to sleep better during the day.

● Try to time her naps well. Having a nap too late in the day can mean that she won't sleep as well at night.

Incidentally, cutting down on daytime naps won't help her to sleep more at night—in fact, it can be a recipe for overtiredness and lead to your baby having a worse night's sleep.

● As soon as you know that your baby is tired, let her sleep. If she gets overtired, she may become irritable and find it very hard to sleep.

● Plan a nap routine to help her wind down. A feeding or drink, a look at a book, and a cuddle before putting her down will be enough.

● Make sure that she has a comfortable place to nap. Letting her fall asleep on your shoulder will be uncomfortable for you, and will mean that she doesn't sleep for long—her crib is better.

● Make sure she isn't too warm or too cold (see pages 56–57).

● Try not to let her fall asleep just before her feeding is due because she will probably wake up too soon out of hunger.

● Change her diaper before you put her down so that she feels comfortable as she settles down.

● Play and interact with your baby when she's awake and active between naps. At five months, she should be able to stay awake for around three hours at a stretch—but with so much to hold her interest now, don't let her get overtired.

Snoring and noisy breathing

From around eight weeks, or sometimes before, some babies start to make "snoring" noises in their sleep. These are caused by loose mucus in the nose and throat (common in young babies) and may be accompanied by a rattling in her chest, which you may be able to feel with your hand. You may also notice a pause in your baby's breathing for a short period.

Some babies have more of a throat gurgle, usually the result of having a soft and flexible airway. This usually resolves itself within a year or two, as the rings of cartilage in the airway become more rigid.

These sounds do not usually interfere with your baby's breathing and will disappear in a few weeks.

Always have any breathing irregularities, snores, gurgles, or pauses in your baby's breathing checked by your healthcare provider. Although it is unlikely to be a serious problem, other causes need to be ruled out. If your baby suddenly starts making strange breathing sounds or wheezes, see your healthcare provider promptly.

" I love it now that Megan's more active during the day, but she gets tired easily. So as soon as she starts rubbing her eyes, I put her down. "

SUE, mother of six-month-old Megan

" I love breastfeeding Eve. I'm also **excited** about giving her some solid food. She already enjoys **sitting with us** at mealtimes. **"**

LIZ, mother of five-month-old Eve

Getting ready for solids

Breast milk is the perfect food for your baby during her first year. But as she grows, milk alone is no longer enough. For healthy physical development, your baby needs to learn how to eat solid food. This is also the first step toward feeding herself and joining in family meals.

Why does your baby need solid food?

As your baby gets bigger, she needs more calories to maintain her growth. If she stays on a diet of breast milk, she'll have to feed more often and her needs will not be satisfied.

Solid food can give your baby the extra calories she needs without filling her up too quickly. It can also give her the extra nutrients her body now requires. For example, from six months on, your baby's natural supply of iron starts to dwindle. Iron is vital for healthy growth, and breast milk cannot provide her with enough.

Introducing your baby to solids is also her first step toward enjoying healthy food and discovering that sharing meals is fun. Your baby is becoming more independent—she is learning how to sit up unaided and to grab what she wants; she loves to put things in her mouth, and she wants to be included in everything.

Learning how to eat solid food and joining in family meals is the next step on her journey to independence.

When to start

The recommended age to start getting your baby used to solids has traditionally been between four and six months. However, experts now believe that babies need nothing more than breast milk for the first six months of their lives. If your baby seems dissatisfied after her usual milk feeding and is less than six months old, try breastfeeding more often, or talk to your healthcare provider. Whether you are breastfeeding or bottle-feeding formula, weaning should start at around six months.

In order for your baby to accept, swallow, and digest solid food, certain physical developments need to occur:
- loss of the tongue-thrust reflex— at birth your baby naturally pushes anything that goes into her mouth

out again with her tongue, but between four and six months this reflex disappears
- development of her jaw and tongue so she can move food to the back of her mouth to swallow
- development of coordination and head control so she can maintain the posture needed for swallowing
- maturity of the gastrointestinal tract so she can digest different foods
- the ability to cope with a larger volume of food in her stomach.

Checklist

Your baby needs to start eating solid food because:

- milk alone can no longer satisfy her physical needs

- her stores of iron are running out and she needs an additional source

- eating solid food is fun—and your baby wants to be part of the family!

Is my baby ready for solids?

Your baby will be ready for solids some time around six months of age. There is no hard and fast rule—as with other skills, such as sitting up or crawling, some babies are ready to move on earlier than others. The deciding factor should be your own baby's needs and development. If you are unsure, talk to your healthcare provider.

Don't start too soon

Until the age of six months, all your baby's nutritional needs are met by your breast milk. Between the ages of four and six months, your baby loses her natural tongue-thrust reflex (see page 79), and as her digestive system matures, she will become able to cope with solid food— waiting until six months is especially important if you have a family history of allergies. Once she is approaching this age, start to watch out for the following signs:

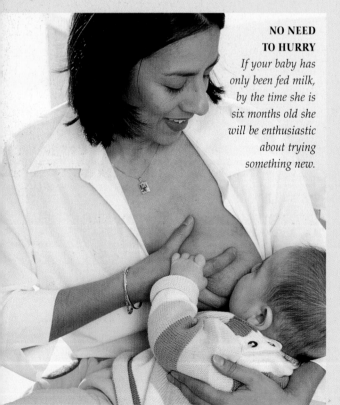

NO NEED TO HURRY
If your baby has only been fed milk, by the time she is six months old she will be enthusiastic about trying something new.

★ **She seems more hungry than usual**
When your baby starts shortening the length of time between feedings or even starts waking in the night for an extra feeding, chances are she could be ready to give solids a try.

★ **She can hold her head up well**
Your baby needs good head control before she can safely be given puréed foods; otherwise, there is a risk of choking. By now, she should be able to lift her head properly when she is propped up or strapped into a reclining chair.

★ **She's interested in the food you eat**
Watch your baby at the table. Is she following each bite you take? Does she look as if she's imitating your chewing? Does she make noises and wave her hands as if saying, "Hey, can I have some?" By six months, most babies are expressing a desire for solid food.

What about premature babies?

If your baby was born early, you need to be careful when calculating her age for starting solids. Avoid introducing them until at least four to six months after her due date rather than after her birthday.

Delaying the introduction of solids much beyond six months may cause problems later on, since teaching older babies to chew can be difficult. In addition, your baby may not be getting all the nutrients she needs from milk alone after this time. Consult your healthcare provider about when to start if you are unsure.

Once you feel your baby is ready to start solids, it's important to go at her pace. Your baby will—like all other babies—discover how to lift her head, swallow purée, and eventually hold her own spoon and feed herself. But she is also unique and will do these things only when she is ready.

Your baby still needs milk

Your baby is not ready to give up the breast or bottle just because she starts eating solid food. At first, she'll simply be getting used to new tastes and textures, and much of what you put in her mouth will come straight back out, so she

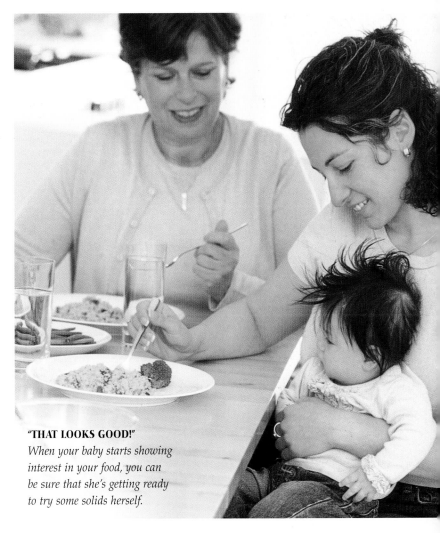

"THAT LOOKS GOOD!"
When your baby starts showing interest in your food, you can be sure that she's getting ready to try some solids herself.

❝ Ben, my oldest, was a hungry baby. Within a few weeks of starting solids, he was devouring everything in sight. Thomas was more laid-back and took longer to get going—but now he loves mealtimes as much as his brother does. ❞

JAN, mother of five-year-old Ben and three-year-old Thomas still needs her full supply of breast milk or formula. In fact, this will be an important source of nutrition for her until she is one year old.

Experiencing solids

For your baby, tasting solids for the first time is an incredible experience. When you offer her these first tastes, you are doing a lot more than just giving her the nourishment she needs—you are stimulating her senses in a way she has never experienced before.

- **Taste**

From an early age, "tasting" is a way of exploring, and as soon as your baby is able, everything within reach will be put in her mouth—although she may not always like the taste! She was born with a full set of 10,000 taste buds and, while they take some years to mature fully, she can already tell the difference between sweet and sour.

- **Smell**

Just as babies prefer sweet tastes, they also prefer sweet smells such

HEAD CONTROL
Your baby's ability to hold his head up without support is a key sign that you will be able to start feeding him solid food before long.

as vanilla and banana. In fact, your baby's sense of smell is so acute that she is able to tell the difference between your breast milk and that of another mother. Smelling is another way in which your baby learns about the world around her—and giving her new foods offers her the chance to discover new smells.

● Touch

Feeling things with her mouth is one of the most important ways your baby has of exploring and learning about her environment. And food teaches her a lot about texture— it can be soft (mashed banana) or hard (a cube of cheese), rough (a rice cracker) or smooth (a grape). Even a runny purée feels strangely different to your baby's mouth, compared with milk.

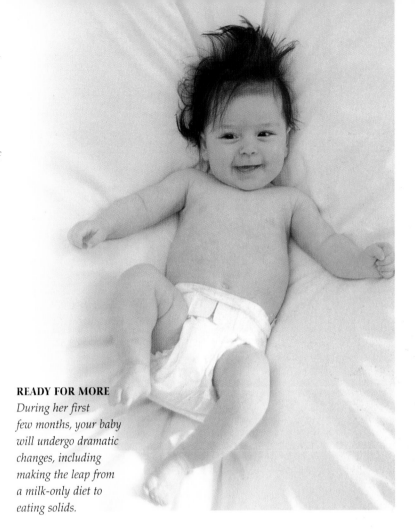

READY FOR MORE
During her first few months, your baby will undergo dramatic changes, including making the leap from a milk-only diet to eating solids.

Questions & Answers

Members of my family suffer from asthma and eczema. Does this affect when I give my baby solids?
Your baby is more likely to be prone to allergies if they run in the family, so it's best to be cautious. Waiting until your baby is at least six months old before introducing solids can help prevent allergies from occurring.

How are allergies caused?
While your baby is young, her digestive tract is more porous, so proteins (the

parts of food that cause allergies) can leak into the bloodstream. Your baby's immune system reacts to these proteins in the way it would react to germs. Then, whenever she eats that particular food, her immune system reacts as if it is an infection. She has what is called an "allergic reaction."

Why does it help to wait until six months before introducing solids?
The older your baby is when she first tastes real food, the more mature her digestive system has become. The proteins are less

likely to leak into the bloodstream and your baby can handle different foods without having an allergic reaction. Also, her immune system is more mature and better at recognizing the difference between food protein and bacteria. Exclusively breastfeeding until your baby is six months old may not stop her from developing an allergy, but it can reduce the likelihood and severity. In babies who have no solids before six months, allergies appear later, tend to be milder, and the children grow out of them earlier.

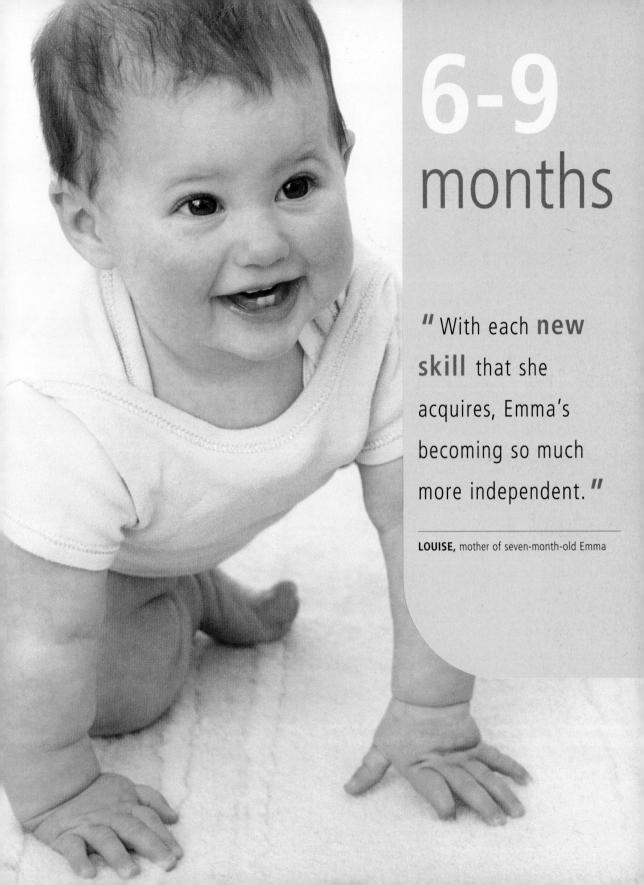

6-9
months

"With each **new skill** that she acquires, Emma's becoming so much more independent."

LOUISE, mother of seven-month-old Emma

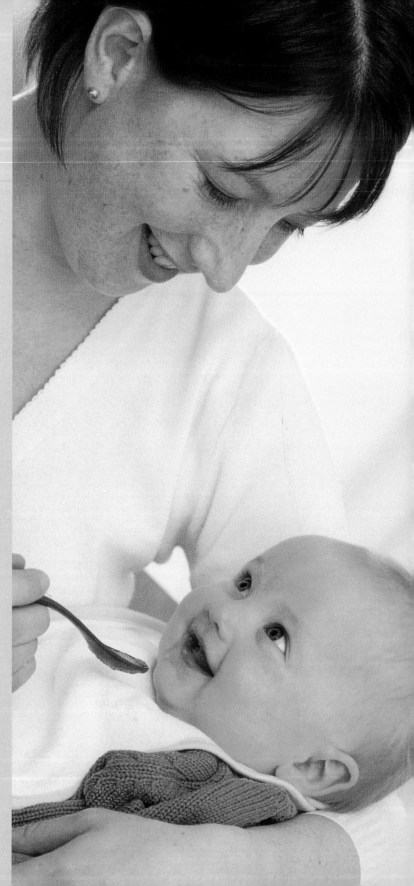

" I'll **never forget** the first time I gave James baby rice cereal— my husband took a **memorable photo** of him smiling at me as he had his first taste of solid food. "

RUTH, mother of six-month-old James

Feeding your baby

Giving your baby his first taste of solid food is an exciting moment. But his first tastes are more about experiencing something new than gaining extra nourishment. Being prepared—knowing which foods to serve and what to expect—will help the moment go smoothly. Here, we look at what you will need and how you can make your baby's first experience of solid food a happy one.

Be prepared

Your baby's first taste of food is a major milestone in his development and one you need to be ready for. Once you decide that the time to introduce solids is approaching, it's worth preparing for the big moment so you can feel calm and in control as you offer your baby his first mouthfuls.

You'll need to make a trip to the store to buy your first few items of baby food. But don't go overboard. Remember, at this stage you are just offering your baby his first tastes of solid food, and it may be a while yet before he's eating three meals a day.

What you will need

For preparing food, you will need:
- a nylon chopping board (wooden boards can harbor germs)
- one of the following for puréeing food, depending on your budget: a nylon or steel sieve and a plastic and nylon or stainless steel spoon; a hand-turned food mill; or a small hand-held electric blender or food processor
- a steamer—good for fast cooking to preserve nutrients
- plastic containers with airtight lids for storing food in the refrigerator
- ice-cube trays for freezing surplus food in convenient small portions
- freezer bags for storing frozen cubes of purée.

For serving food, you will need:
- lots of soft fabric bibs (easy to wear and easy to wash) and a plastic bib with a curved bottom designed to catch food (especially useful once your baby starts feeding himself)
- a set of plastic bowls—unbreakable and easy to wash
- plastic teaspoons with soft or round edges—easier on tender gums.

Where should my baby sit?

You can sit your baby on your lap or strap him into his baby seat or car seat, preferably placed on the floor for safety. If he still can't sit up unaided, he will need to be slightly reclined—but he should be upright enough to eat and swallow without choking.

Great expectations

Lots of parents have a camera ready to record the moment when their baby has his first taste of solid food—but don't expect too much! Remember that this is the first time your baby has tasted anything other than milk.

The new taste and texture will probably baffle him, and chances are that what goes in—if anything does—will end up rolling right back out again!

Learning to eat food takes time and practice. Your baby will go at his own pace, but there is plenty you can do to encourage his interest in food.

● Let him sit on your lap at family meals so he can see everyone enjoying their food.

● As he becomes more adept at using his hands, he'll love playing with his food. Let him squish a piece of cooked pasta or dip his hands in some yogurt.

● Talk to him while you are preparing his food—whether you are getting ready to breastfeed, fixing a bottle, or getting his solids ready.

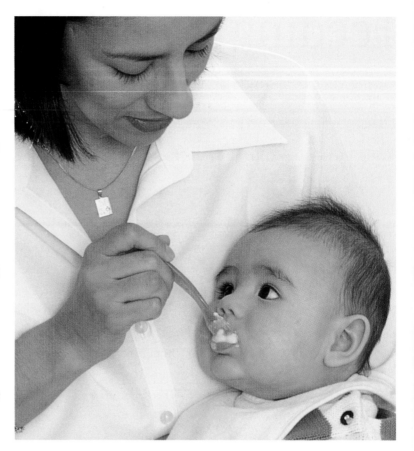

How to give the first feeding

● Talking to your baby the whole time, prepare a small amount of food using the methods described on page 92. Then give him up to half of his usual milk feeding to take the edge off his appetite.

● Sit him on your lap or in a baby seat or car seat. Using a plastic spoon, place a tiny amount of food in between his lips. Don't push it in too far or your baby may gag. And don't worry if he pushes it right back out—he'll soon learn how to suck food from the spoon. A tiny amount will stay in his mouth, and you can scoop the remainder up and slip it back in.

● Give your baby lots of loving attention—chat, smile, tell him how wonderful he is. Make a point of touching him

and stroking him whenever you can to help him feel safe and secure.

● Try another spoonful, but don't expect him to take more than a couple of tiny teaspoons. Don't worry if most of it ends up smeared around his face—he's discovering what it feels like and is more likely to let you try again if he is having fun.

● Once your baby has had enough, he'll turn his head away, close his mouth, or lean back.

● Tell him how good he is and give him lots of cuddles. Finish up with the remainder of his milk feeding if he's interested.

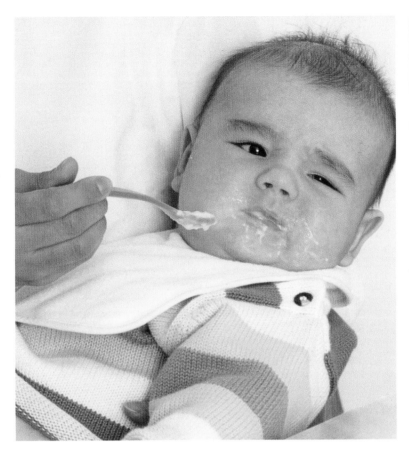

A WHOLE NEW EXPERIENCE
At first, give your baby only tiny amounts of food at a time. When he has had enough, he will close his mouth and turn his head away.

Tell him what you are doing and praise him for watching. He'll love the attention and learn to associate mealtimes with happy occasions.

A new skill to learn

Once you've decided that today is the day for giving your baby a taste of something new, get everything ready beforehand and choose a time when you are both feeling happy and relaxed. Introducing new foods takes time, so it may be worth putting on the answering machine and forgetting about other chores while you give your baby your full attention.

Most babies make faces from surprise no matter how much they like the new tastes. So how do you know whether your baby loves or loathes the food you are giving him?
• If he likes it, he'll open his mouth for more, in which case you can continue to offer him a few teaspoons each day, gradually increasing the thickness of the purées.
• If he doesn't like it, he'll turn his head away, cry, or seem uninterested.

Don't worry—chances are today is just not the day. Try again tomorrow. If your baby still isn't eager, wait a few days and give it another try. If he's still not interested, talk to your healthcare provider.

Don't be worried if your baby is finding it hard to get the hang of eating solid food—until now he has always taken his food by sucking, and learning how to feed from a spoon takes lots of practice. His tongue-thrust reflex (see page 79) is only just starting to disappear and

Trying new tastes

Some babies are naturally reluctant to try new tastes. Here are some ideas to help you both:

● Serve your baby's food at room temperature or only slightly warmed.

● If your baby rejects the spoon, dip a clean finger into the food and let him suck the food from it.

● Try offering some food after a shorter breast- or bottle-feed than usual. If he's alert but not overhungry, he may be more eager.

● Don't prepare too much—one advantage of ready-to-mix baby rice cereal is that it provides tiny servings without wasting food.

often the food you give your baby will simply dribble out because he doesn't know how to get it far enough back on his tongue to swallow.

Give him only a tiny bit of food, holding the spoon close to his lips. If he likes what he tastes, he'll soon discover that by sucking he can draw the food off the spoon. Sucking will also help him get the food to the back of his mouth so he can swallow it.

When your baby has had enough, he'll close his mouth or turn his head away. No matter how much is left in his bowl, don't force him to eat any more—your baby needs to decide for himself whether he's still hungry and which foods he likes. And while,

at this stage, it's hard to tell whether he's rejecting a new taste because he doesn't like it or is still mastering the art of eating, it's better to be cautious than pushy.

What to avoid

Never add any of the following to your baby's food:

● salt—this can overload his kidneys

● sugar—this can encourage a sweet tooth

● honey, in liquid or solid form— it can contain spores that cause infant botulism: the digestive systems of babies under one year old are immature, and the spores can grow there and cause life-threatening illness.

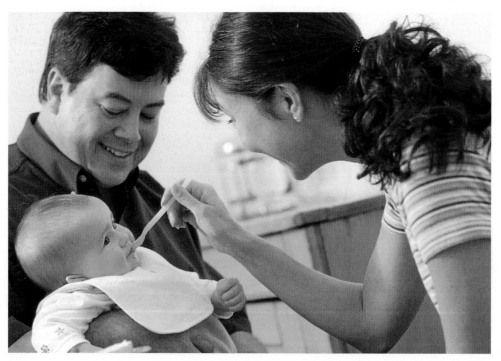

DAD'S TURN
Starting on solids provides a great opportunity for dad to get involved with feeding.

PASTA PLAY
Allowing your baby to handle solid food will help him explore and get used to different shapes and textures.

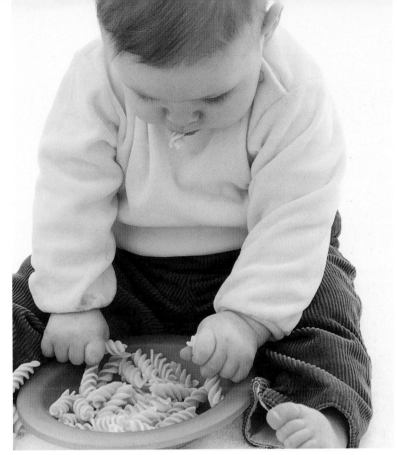

Don't be tempted to mix baby rice cereal into your baby's bottle. Adding cereal to bottles risks overfeeding your baby and can cause choking. Also, it's important that your baby gets used to the mechanics of eating: taking a spoonful, resting, taking another, and stopping when he's full. Experiencing his first foods in this way will help your child develop good eating habits that will last a lifetime.

Diaper changes

Once your baby starts eating solids, you will notice changes in the consistency and color of his stools. They will be more solid, darker, and probably smellier! This may come as a bit of a shock—especially if up until now your baby has been totally breastfed and his diapers fairly inoffensive. The change is perfectly normal. His digestive system is still immature and the food often doesn't change much between going in and coming out again.

If your baby's stools become hard, you notice him straining, or he passes fewer stools per day, talk to your healthcare provider—your baby may be constipated.

Questions & Answers

When's the best time of day to give my baby his first foods?
Your baby needs to be relaxed, not too hungry, and not too tired. Early morning and late evening may not be the best times, since your baby might be hungry, half awake, or half asleep. He may be more cooperative midmorning and in late afternoon. Watch him closely and feed him when he's happy, hasn't had a milk feeding for a while, but isn't too hungry.

Will starting my baby on solid food help him sleep through the night?
Lots of parents imagine that introducing their babies to solids will help them sleep through the night. Research shows that this isn't the case. Babies routinely wake in the night—even when they are not hungry—and until they learn how to comfort themselves and fall back to sleep on their own, they are unable to sleep for extended periods of time.

My baby just isn't interested in solids. What should I do?
It's much more important at this stage that both of you enjoy mealtimes, and if, despite your best efforts, your baby isn't eager to give solids a try, don't force the issue. Instead, go back to breast- or bottle-feeding for a few days, then try again. If you have concerns, talk to your healthcare provider.

How should I prepare my baby's food?

Preparing simple purées made from fruits and vegetables for your baby doesn't take long—and it's less expensive than store-bought baby food. With a few simple precautions and cooking tips, you can give your baby safe and healthy meals. You can also easily prepare small quantities in advance so they are ready when your baby needs to be fed.

Making your own purées

Try to cook fresh fruit and vegetables within a day or so of buying them.

1 Wash and prepare the fruit or vegetable and cut into even-sized pieces.

2 Steam or boil (use as little water as possible to preserve the nutrients).

3 When soft, allow the food to cool a little, then purée it using a hand mill, food processor, or hand-held blender. Alternatively, you can push it through a sieve.

4 Test the temperature of the food on your fingertip or arm before giving it to your baby—room temperature or slightly warm is best. Babies' palates are very sensitive, so be careful not to burn your baby's mouth.

HEALTHY COOKING
Using a steamer to cook your baby's food will help preserve the nutrients that are normally lost during the cooking process.

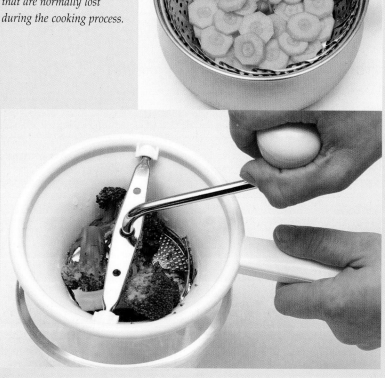

PURÉEING YOUR BABY'S FOOD
A hand-operated food mill is ideal for puréeing your baby's cooked food. This stage won't last for long, so don't buy an electric blender just for this purpose.

PREPARE IN ADVANCE
You can have home-cooked baby food always on hand if you make a large quantity of purée in advance and freeze spoonfuls of it in a sterilized ice-cube tray.

Freezing and storing

At this stage, your baby is only tasting a tiny amount of food. Unused purée can be spooned into a sterilized ice-cube tray and frozen until needed. You can also freeze ahead—make a large amount of purée, spoon it into a sterilized ice-cube tray, and freeze until the cubes are solid. Dump the cubes into a plastic bag, then seal and label it before returning it to the freezer. Individual cubes can then be removed and defrosted in the refrigerator in a bowl or on a plate. Heat thoroughly as and when required.

You can sterilize a freshly washed ice-cube tray by washing it in the dishwasher or putting it in a pan of boiling water for 5 to 10 minutes.

Food hygiene

Food poisoning is easy to prevent. Make eating safe for your baby by taking the following precautions:

★ wash your hands carefully before feeding your baby—especially if you have been handling raw food

HANDY NUTRITION
When frozen, take the cubes of puréed food out of the tray and store in sealed freezer bags, one type of food per bag. Carefully label and date each bag and use within three months of freezing.

★ keep kitchen equipment and work spaces as clean as possible

★ don't save leftovers from the bowl your baby has just used—bacteria will grow and any enzymes from your baby's saliva will thin the food out

★ if you are using a ready-made jar of food, remove as much as you need rather than feeding directly from the jar, unless you are finishing the jar off

★ if you are heating your baby's food, heat only enough for one meal and discard any leftovers

★ refrigerate cold food for no more than 24 hours, and use warm food as soon as it's ready.

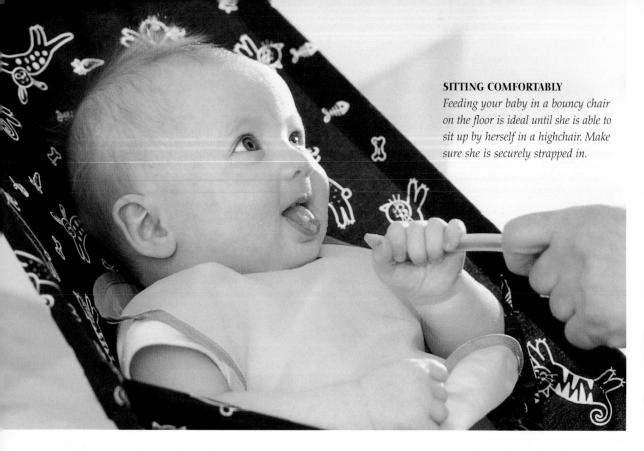

" I always prepare Daniel's purée before I breastfeed him. He loves sitting in his chair watching me. I'm sure he's finishing on the breast quicker so he can get to his solid food sooner!"

SIMONE, mother of six-month-old Daniel

Some time around her six-month birthday you can give your baby her first taste of solid food. If she likes it you can build up to two or three mini-meals a day. Over the next few weeks you can start introducing a wider variety, but it's important to take your time, and watch out for allergic reactions.

Once she is eating two or three spoonfuls of baby cereal or a homemade purée every day, try a different single food. Don't be worried if she doesn't accept it right away. It's perfectly normal to have to offer a new food between 10 and 20 times before it's accepted. Once your baby clearly likes the taste, give this

new food exclusively for at least a couple of days before trying another.

Offering one food at a time, and only one new food every two or three days, has two advantages: Your baby can get used to each new taste and texture, and if there are any signs of an allergic reaction—such as a stomachache, diarrhea, or rashes—you will be able to identify very quickly which food was the culprit.

First purées to try include carrots, parsnips, rutabagas, sweet potatoes, cooked apples, and mashed bananas. Once your baby is happy taking semi-liquid food from a spoon, gradually start to thicken the purée or cereal by adding less liquid. This allows your baby to practice her chewing and swallowing skills and will help ease the transition from purées to lumpier food.

If your baby has a reaction

Although some foods are more likely than others to cause problems, any food can potentially trigger an allergic reaction. Food allergies that affect the immune system are rare, but some children find certain foods more difficult to tolerate than others and may have a reaction.

If you think your baby had a reaction to a particular food, wait a couple of weeks before trying it again. The same reaction two or three times would suggest that your baby is sensitive and you should wait a few months before reintroducing it. Most babies eventually grow out of this kind of food problem. Consult your healthcare provider if you are unsure.

Food combinations

Once your baby has eaten several single foods with no adverse reaction, mix two foods together. Combinations that work well include broccoli and sweet potatoes, carrots and parsnips, and stewed apples and pears.

Milk needs at six months

Once your baby is happily having two or three solid "meals" a day with milk in between (even if the "meals" consist of only a couple of spoonfuls at each serving), you may find that she's not feeding as much from the breast or bottle. Usually, early morning and pre-bedtime feedings stay the same, but during the day your baby may nurse a little less or take a little less formula.

● **Good for nutrition** Although your baby is starting to eat real food, milk is still an essential part of her diet. Purées offer little in the way of extra calories—and calories are what your baby needs to maintain her growth and weight gain. Until her daily menu incorporates three proper meals, she still needs around 20 fl oz (600ml) of milk a day. If you are breastfeeding, it's impossible to check, but if you let her take the lead, she'll probably get what she needs. If you have concerns, talk to your healthcare provider.

● **Good for comfort** Although your baby is starting to recognize that solids can satisfy hunger as well as milk, sucking is still a way of feeling close to you. Your baby loves nothing better than feeling safe and secure in your arms, and breastfeeding or bottle-feeding her is still important as a way of giving her comfort.

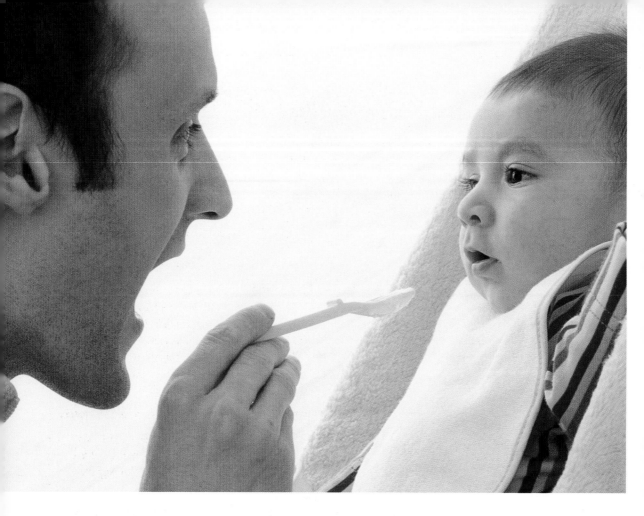

What is gluten?

Gluten is a protein found in wheat, barley, rye, and perhaps oats. Sensitivity to gluten can trigger celiac disease. In a small number of babies, when the intestine comes in contact with gluten, an allergic reaction occurs and the intestine's lining becomes smooth, preventing nutrients from being properly absorbed, and this is associated with permanent intolerance to gluten. Symptoms include stomach pain, diarrhea, weight loss, irritability, and nausea.

Foods that contain gluten, such as bread, pasta, and crackers, should never be given to babies under six months. Once your baby is six months old, her intestines are less likely to develop gluten intolerance.

If celiac disease is diagnosed, your child will need to eat a gluten-free diet for life. She'll be referred to a dietician who can advise you what she can and can't eat. Nowadays, larger supermarkets stock gluten-free alternatives, including bread, biscuits, cereals, and pasta.

WATCH AND LEARN
Open your mouth as you offer your baby her food, and she will probably open hers in response.

Store-bought baby food

There are many advantages to making your own baby food—it's cheap, easy, and your baby can get used to the types of food your family normally eats. But there are times when ready-made jars are more convenient—for example, when you are traveling. You can choose from many different flavors and ingredients, and the foods are usually categorized according to age. They don't contain salt but some have added sugar and modified starch, so read the list of ingredients carefully. Always be sure to:

- check the expiration date on the container
- store unopened jars in a cool place
- make sure the vacuum seal button is down—don't use a jar if the button has popped up
- don't feed your baby directly from the jar—take out the amount of food she needs and serve it separately
- once opened, keep the jar with its contents in the refrigerator—it should stay fresh for one to two days, but always read the label.

Are organic fruits and vegetables best?

Many people worry about the effects on children's health of pesticides and other chemicals used to produce food. Organic fruits and vegetables are grown in soil fertilized with manure and compost instead of synthetic chemicals. Research has shown, however, that levels of pesticides in fruits and vegetables are typically well below the safety levels set by government agencies. You can take extra care with your child's health by washing fruits and vegetables thoroughly before cooking and serving.

Foods to avoid at six months

Advice on which foods are suitable for your baby can sometimes change, so check also with your healthcare provider. But as a general guideline, you should not give the following foods to babies who are six months old:

- **nuts and nut products, especially those containing peanuts:** for babies with a family history of allergies, continue to avoid these up to the age of three; whole nuts should not be given to children until age seven or older because of the risk of choking

- **foods that carry a higher risk of food poisoning:** these include mold-ripened cheeses, liver pâté, and soft-boiled eggs (up to the age of nine months, only egg yolk should be given, since this is the high-nutrition part of the egg, and whites are more likely to cause allergies)

- **salt:** your baby's kidneys are too immature to cope with this

- **sugar, honey, or other sweeteners:** these can lead to a sweet tooth and honey can also contain a potentially dangerous spore (see page 90)—if you need to, sweeten desserts with mashed bananas instead

- **soft drinks:** these may contain high levels of artificial sweeteners; offer cooled boiled water or occasionally diluted unsweetened fruit juice at mealtimes if you want to give your baby an alternative to milk

- **tea:** this can reduce iron absorption

- **low–fat and high–fiber foods:** babies need more calories and less bulk to give them the energy they need to grow

- **processed foods:** these contain too much salt.

Every baby is different

Your baby may take a couple of weeks to get the hang of solids. This is fine, as long as she is drinking plenty of milk to meet her nutritional needs.

On the other hand, your baby may race ahead and manage two or three "meals" a day in no time at all. If she is happily eating solids, coping well with taking food from a spoon, and enjoying a wide range of fruit and vegetable purées, you may wish to start gradually introducing other foods such as red meat, poultry, lentils, or split peas to her purées.

Remember that your baby's digestive system is still adjusting to solid food, so add only small quantities of new foods—and still just one at a time in case she has an allergic reaction. You may find that it takes longer for your baby to accept meat and poultry, so purée a tiny amount with her favorite vegetable.

When is the best time to start giving my baby finger foods?

Every day your baby is getting better at using his hands and fingers, and this makes it easier for him to try things such as feeding himself. His hand–eye coordination is improving by leaps and bounds, and now he can pick up a piece of food and then put it into his mouth—although not without making a bit of a mess!

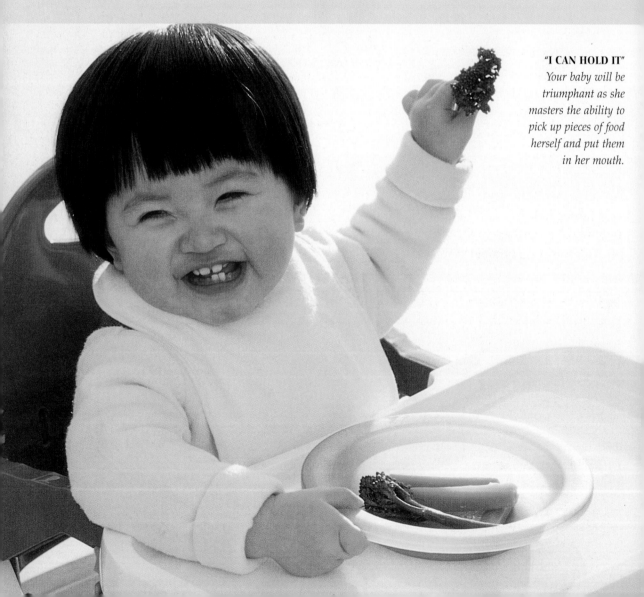

"I CAN HOLD IT"
Your baby will be triumphant as she masters the ability to pick up pieces of food herself and put them in her mouth.

Getting started

Most babies are ready for finger food by about seven months. For a while, your baby will hold the food in his fist and work hard to push in the last mouthful using the flat of his hand. Over the next few months, however, he'll start to pick up things using his thumb and forefinger, a skill called the pincer grasp. In time, this will allow him to pick up tiny pieces of food such as raisins or peas.

Your baby can easily choke from eating too fast or putting too much into his mouth. Stay close—and never leave your baby alone at mealtimes.

Learning to chew

Practicing chewing is important, and not only because it means your baby can eat a wider range of foods. Chewing also helps your baby practice moving his mouth and tongue in preparation for speech. Your baby is using his gums to chew, so choose foods that can be gummed to a soft consistency or will dissolve in his mouth without chewing. Here are some ideas:

★ cubes of bread, rice cakes, or toast
★ dry cereals
★ chunks of soft fruit, such as banana or melon
★ small pieces of cooked vegetables, such as carrots, broccoli, or cauliflower
★ well-cooked pasta, cut down in size if necessary
★ tiny cubes of hard cheese.

PREPARING FINGER FOOD
Even if your baby has some teeth, he'll still use his gums to chew for a while. Always cut food into manageable chunks, and don't offer him too much at a time. He might just try to stuff it all in at once—or sweep it all onto the floor!

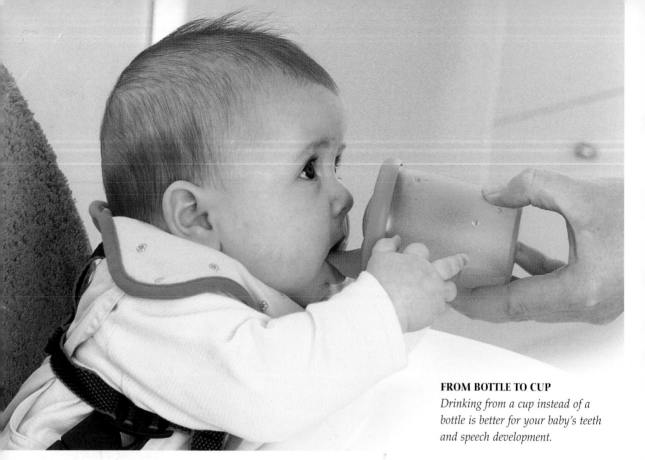

FROM BOTTLE TO CUP
Drinking from a cup instead of a bottle is better for your baby's teeth and speech development.

Seven to nine months

As the number of foods you can give your baby rapidly expands, mealtimes will become easier as he starts to enjoy some of the same foods as you do. Over the next few months, your baby will be building up to three regular meals a day with two or three snacks in between. He'll now be sitting up on his own for extended periods, and will be eager to get more involved in feeding himself. Giving him his own spoon and offering him finger foods will encourage him to try more substantial foods, which, in turn, will help him develop chewing skills.

Foods to avoid at seven to nine months

At this age there are still certain foods that are not suitable for your baby. Continue to avoid:

- **adding salt, sugar, and honey:** use mashed bananas for sweetening desserts instead

- **nuts:** avoid all nuts and nut products, especially if your family is known to have a history of allergies

- **foods that present a choking hazard:** these include whole grapes, nuts, large pieces of apple or raw carrots, uncooked peas, and celery

- **soft drinks:** they may contain high levels of artificial sweeteners; offer cooled boiled water and occasionally diluted fruit juice at mealtimes if you want an alternative to milk

- **foods that carry a higher risk of food poisoning:** these include as mold-ripened cheeses, liver pâté, and soft-boiled eggs (up to the age of nine months, only yolk should be given since this is the high-nutrition part of an egg, and whites are more likely to cause allergies)

- **low-fat and high-fiber foods:** babies need more calories and less bulk to give them the energy they need to grow

- **processed foods:** these contain too much salt.

Calories

Your baby still needs plenty of calories for energy and growth. Introducing a wider variety of food into his diet helps a lot. But to make sure your baby is getting enough protein, calcium, and vitamins at around 7–9 months, you should still give him about 17–20 fl oz (500–600ml) of formula or two full breastfeedings every day.

Advancing to a cup

Your baby will naturally feel thirsty while he's eating. This is a good time to introduce a cup so that he can take sips of water or fruit juice during mealtimes. Be sure to limit the amount of juice he drinks to 4 fl oz (120ml) a day and dilute it by at least one part juice to three parts water.

● Choose a nondrip, soft-spout cup for first-timers. Some babies prefer a cup with one or two handles; others prefer no handles.

● Help your baby by holding the cup to his mouth and tipping it for him to show him how it works.

● Expect your baby just to play with it at first. This is all part of the learning process.

● Avoid letting him carry it around with him—offer it to him only while he is in his high chair.

Foods your baby can eat

Your baby is now ready for a whole range of tastes and can share many of your family meals, provided no sugar or salt has been added. Remember to introduce new tastes and textures gradually.

Try to include at least one protein-based meal a day—fish, meat, egg yolks, lentils, or beans—since these are good sources of protein and iron. Iron is particularly important—by the time your baby is six months old, the iron stores with which he was born are starting to dwindle, and milk alone will not satisfy all his daily requirements (see page 79).

Make sure your baby also has a portion each of fruit, vegetables, and starchy food every day, too. He can also eat foods containing gluten, so try white or whole-wheat bread, pasta, or couscous.

And you can now use cow's milk in meals—added to cereal, for example.

Protein
- beans and legumes
- cheese
- chicken or turkey
- cow's milk in meals (e.g., with cereal)
- boneless fish
- red meat
- tofu
- eggs (yolks only, since their nutritional value is higher and they are less likely to cause allergies than whites)

Fruit
- grapes (cut in half and seeds removed)
- oranges (seedless)
- mangoes
- melons
- tangerines (seedless)
- strawberries
- pieces of pear

Vegetables
- butternut squash
- cucumber
- green beans
- leeks
- peas
- mushrooms
- onions
- sweetcorn

Starchy food
- potatoes
- bread
- noodles
- rice
- pasta
- couscous
- breakfast cereals
- oatmeal

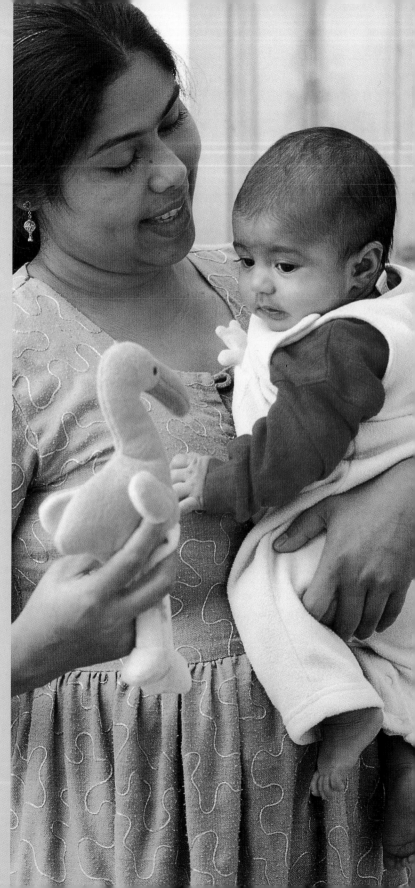

" Natasha doesn't like being left alone—that always makes her cry. I **comfort her** by picking her up and rubbing her back, and saying, **'It's okay.'** Then I find something to amuse her. "

JENNIFER, mother of four-month-old Natasha

Crying in older babies

From around three to six months of age, your baby will begin to cry less. Even babies who have cried excessively should show signs of settling down by six months. You're more confident now because you are more in tune with your baby, and have developed many effective ways of soothing her.

A turning point

Many babies just grow out of crying excessively, often by around three months. This is partly related to your baby's development. She's now becoming more sociable and is able to do more on her own—for example, she can now roll over and grasp toys with her hands.

It is also because your older baby is more adept at finding ways of soothing herself. She can now find and suck her own thumb, and may start becoming attached to a "transitional" comfort object.

It is true that a few babies who did not seem to cry excessively in the early days begin to cry more at around five to six months. This may be caused by teething or distress at the introduction of solid foods. It is also a possibility that they need to cry more to ensure more interaction with their parents, who may have been providing them

with less attention because they seemed so much more settled! Either way, you have learned so much over these last months about handling your baby, finding out her likes and dislikes, that you now deal easily with her needs. You have a better understanding of the different patterns of her crying. You will probably have many effective ways of comforting her.

More good news!

By now, family life is settling into a more comfortable routine. You know how to keep her happy a lot more of the time, and it's rewarding when she takes an interest in toys or watches you contentedly from a sitting position while you carry out jobs around the house. This in turn means that there is a much wider range of activities you can try to calm her when she does cry.

Checklist

All babies cry less after three months. This is partly for developmental reasons, but is also because:

- she's taking an interest in the world around her, so there's more to see and do

- she's more active and is busy developing her motor skills

- she's more sociable and is better able to interact with you and other caregivers

- you know your baby well by now and can recognize her crying triggers

- you have more effective ways of soothing her crying.

Why older babies cry

Hunger, overstimulation, and overtiredness are still likely causes for your older baby's crying. You will probably be familiar with the signs to look out for now and be ready to comfort her.

However, there are now a number of new reasons why your older babymay cry:

● Crying for attention

Older babies can cry intentionally, because they want you to come to them, and then act pleased to see you. It is wrong to think of this as "naughty" behavior or manipulation. She still uses crying as a means of communicating her needs and emotions. Also, there is no one in the world as important to your baby as you are. She wants to spend time with you, and demonstrates this by squealing with delight whenever you come to her. This is part of the magic of parenting.

● Starting solid foods

You may notice more crying at mealtimes when your baby is trying her first solids at around six months. This could be because your baby simply dislikes the new feeding experience or the taste of the food. She may reject a cup or spoon, or object to having to wait for her milk after her meal.

● Boredom

The chances of your baby's feeling bored can increase as she grows older and spends less time sleeping during the day, so that bouncing seats, toys, mobiles, and your company all become increasingly important to keep her occupied for parts of the day.

● Anxiety and fright

Your older baby may start to worry about things that never bothered her before. Typically, it may be the sound of the vacuum cleaner, or the sight of an animal, or having hair washed that starts the crying.

Even if these fears seem trivial to you, you must not let her know that.

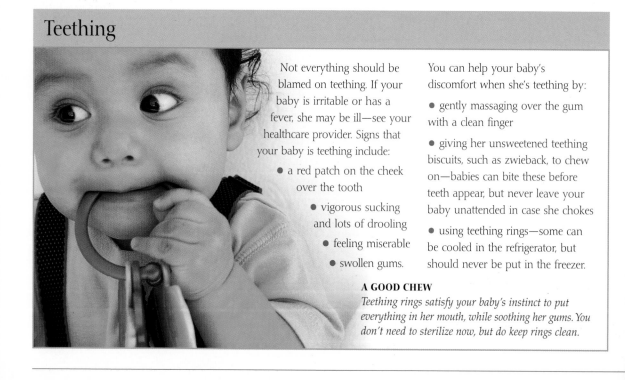

Teething

Not everything should be blamed on teething. If your baby is irritable or has a fever, she may be ill—see your healthcare provider. Signs that your baby is teething include:

● a red patch on the cheek over the tooth

● vigorous sucking and lots of drooling

● feeling miserable

● swollen gums.

You can help your baby's discomfort when she's teething by:

● gently massaging over the gum with a clean finger

● giving her unsweetened teething biscuits, such as zwieback, to chew on—babies can bite these before teeth appear, but never leave your baby unattended in case she chokes

● using teething rings—some can be cooled in the refrigerator, but should never be put in the freezer.

A GOOD CHEW
Teething rings satisfy your baby's instinct to put everything in her mouth, while soothing her gums. You don't need to sterilize now, but do keep rings clean.

Separation anxiety

Having spent all the early months of her life becoming attached to you, it is very common for your baby not to want to let you out of her sight from about seven to eight months. Often, this new behavior coincides with the time when you need to introduce childcare for the first time, perhaps because you are returning to work.

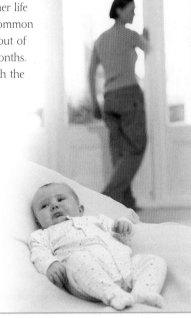

Some babies will be more "clingy" than others, considering everyone other than Mommy or Daddy to be a "stranger"—even grandparents. Be patient with this phase. You are the center of her universe, and she doesn't yet understand the concept of time, or know that when you leave her, you will definitely be coming back.

Your baby needs plenty of loving sympathy, because these fears seem very important to her.

● Loss of a comfort object

Your baby may have become very attached to a security object, such as a pacifier, a soft toy, or even a scrap of cloth. It can cause great distress and crying if this object gets lost or mislaid, most often in her crib during the night.

Make sure you have a spare one in case the precious original is lost for good, and always remember to take the comfort object with you whenever you are out or staying away from home.

● Frustration

As your baby grows, she inevitably wants to try to do more. She may attempt to crawl before she's quite ready, or struggle to grab an interesting-looking toy that's just out of her reach, and is likely to cry when she realizes that she can't manage to do everything—or have everything—that she wants. She needs lots of help and comfort from you to keep this frustration from becoming overwhelming.

● Bumps and bruises

Once on the move, babies can hurt themselves in lots of ways that younger babies can't, and the

Expert tips

The following will help your baby cope with separation anxiety.

● Talk to her whenever you're out of sight—"Here I am! I'll be back soon!"—or sing a song, so that she knows you're still there.

● Use games, such as peekaboo (popping out from behind the door, or even just covering your face with your hands). You are teaching her "object permanence"—that a person can go and come back, and is still there even though she can't be seen.

● Move her to wherever you are if possible, and let her watch you—she will come out of this phase sooner if she is not left alone feeling anxious.

● When you must leave a room briefly, try to involve her in an activity before you go.

● Set aside times to give her your undivided loving attention—cuddling up with a book or playing a game—since this helps security grow.

● If you have to leave her with another caregiver, such as a babysitter, or at daycare, take it slowly, giving her time to get used to the idea. Never sneak away—this will upset her more. For sensitive children, even a short separation may need extra effort—explaining in advance, allowing lots of time for the handover, reassuring her that you will be back.

● Give your child something of yours that has your smell on it—a T-shirt, for example.

Questions & Answers

What are nightmares and night terrors?

Many children have nightmares, but a few may wake up crying from them. They happen in the lighter, dreaming (REM) phase of sleep, and older children can usually remember them in the morning. Reassure your baby and settle her back to sleep.

Night terrors are less common. They occur during deep sleep, and are not remembered after waking. They can be frightening for parents to witness. Your baby may be screaming and thrashing around, but she will not be awake and therefore won't know what is happening. It is often better not to attempt to wake her up, but to try to gently soothe her, perhaps whispering, "It's OK, I'm here. Don't be scared," and touching her gently.

If your baby's night terrors really worry you, try to spot a pattern. For example, if they happen three hours after your baby goes to sleep, try to rouse her shortly before that time. Hopefully, you'll be able to put her back to sleep again and intercept the event. Your baby will grow out of night terrors without any harmful or long-term effects.

resulting bumps and knocks can lead to more tears. Plan ahead to childproof your home as your baby becomes more mobile. As well as protecting her from accidents, it can save frustration in the early years. Babies and toddlers do not have the ability to remember the word "No!" and repeating it can sometimes reinforce bad behavior. With the freedom to explore safely, you will avoid having to repeat it to her until she is old enough to understand.

● "Whining" and "fussing"

This type of crying can be common in some older babies, while others may never do it. It can help to treat this as your baby's "conversation" and talk back to her, saying for example, "You're probably feeling bored going around this store," or "You don't like sitting in that car seat, do you?" Anything interesting to create a distraction—for example, giving her a set of keys to jangle—will keep her amused for a while.

● Night crying

By around the age of three months, most babies can sleep for five-hour stretches at night, but one-third of babies still wake at one year, so there is wide variation, and a lot of babies will still be waking and crying in the night (see page 108).

ON THE MOVE
Whether she's rolling, crawling, or already up on her feet, your older baby is likely to cry more from frustration or as a result of bumps as she struggles to perfect her skills.

WHERE IS SHE?
*Peekaboo is more
than just a game.
It teaches
your baby "object
permanence"—that
someone she loves
is still there, even
though she can't
see her.*

Settling down to sleep

You may have already started establishing ways to teach your baby to
settle herself down to sleep (see pages 71–77). From four months, such
routines become important both for daytime naps and at bedtime.

• At the age of four months, your baby will need two daytime naps of two
to three hours each. By nine months, these will probably be reduced to one
to two hours each. It's best to try to put her down for these naps while she's
still awake and at roughly the same time each day.

• Continue keeping bedtimes peaceful. Set up a calm "winding down" period
with a recognizable routine, such as a bath, song, or bedtime story, so that
your baby always knows that "sleep time" is coming up.

• Aim to put her down in her crib while she's drowsy but still awake, so that
she learns how it feels to fall asleep on her own and develops her own self-
soothing strategies. She's also less likely to wake in the night and cry, because
her surroundings are familiar and she can go back to sleep by herself.

• Reconsider any comforting routines you have been using so far, such as
giving her a pacifier, lying down with her, or stroking her to settle her down.
From four months onward, your baby will expect these as part of her
routine, and once firmly established, they will be hard to change.

New challenges

It's important to allow your baby
plenty of time to adjust slowly to
any changes in her routine, whether
it's her first taste of solid food or a
new childcare arrangement. Despite
her developing maturity, it is asking
too much of your baby to expect
her to happily accept major changes
overnight without some protest.

You will avoid unnecessary tears if
you are always sympathetic to your
baby's fears. Give her plenty of hugs
and loving attention to help her deal
with them. Many babies take a while
to adjust to new situations, and your
baby is likely to need patient
understanding from you for some
time to come.

Questions & Answers

My eight-month-old son had been sleeping through the night until about 6:00 am for some time. But for the last week or two he's started waking and crying at least twice during the night. Why is this?

It is quite common for a baby who had begun to show signs of sleeping through the night to start waking and crying again at around eight to nine months. Babies this age might be more easily disturbed because they're more aware of their surroundings, and they may also find it harder to go back to sleep without you to help them. Your baby may have become very attached to a particular method of going to sleep, whether it involves sucking a pacifier, holding a toy, or being cuddled, so he may need this reassurance again when he wakes up at night—or even several times a night. Help him develop better sleep habits (see right) and see if you can settle him back into a good nighttime routine in which he can fall back to sleep on his own.

Night waking

Up to about six months of age, your baby will probably wake during the night. She may still wake to be fed during these times, but beyond six months, if she wakes it is more likely to be because she wants comfort or because something has disturbed her. Night waking can also be a sign of growth spurts—both physical and developmental.

Waking up in the dark can make her puzzled and frightened, and if she is unable to settle herself back to sleep, she will start crying for you.

It's quite common from this age for babies who have been sleeping through the night for some time to start a new phase of night waking (see *Questions & Answers*, left).

We all stir from time to time during the night as we move between states of quiet and active (REM) sleep, but most of the time we're able simply to drift off to sleep again. Babies need to learn how to do this, and there are ways in which you can encourage your baby to develop good sleep habits.

● Resist going in to your baby at the first whimper. She may just be stirring, and if you leave her for a minute or two, she may stop crying and go back to sleep on her own.

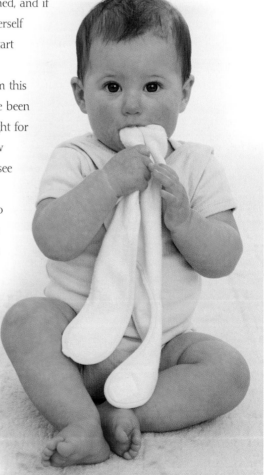

> **"** *Jack's cuddly blanket has a magical effect. He stops crying as soon as I hand it to him.* **"**
>
> **NEIL,** father of eight-month-old Jack

● You may want to try methods to encourage better sleep (see below), which are taught by some health professionals to help parents manage their babies' crying and sleeplessness. The aim is to help your baby settle down to sleep at bedtime and when she wakes at night.

● Try to avoid lifting her from the crib when she wakes (see below) but, if you have to, keep the room dark. Speak quietly or rock her soothingly. You are aiming to help her understand that nighttime is for sleeping, not for playing.

● If she regularly wakes at night, there could be something disturbing her. Check that she's not too hot or too cold and that her room is not too bright or too dark. Consider also

whether she's being woken by a noise—perhaps she hears you stirring if she's still sleeping in your room.

● Try to keep reminding yourself that these night-waking episodes are a very short time in a child's

life. If you can deal patiently with your baby now, she will eventually feel secure in the knowledge that you or your partner will always come to her when you are needed to answer calls of distress.

Encouraging better sleep

"Sleep training" can encourage your older baby to settle down on her own, safe in the knowledge that you are there but understanding that her waking will not be rewarded with a cuddle or a feeding.

Allow at least a week for it to start taking effect, and you may need to be prepared for things to get worse before they start getting better. Share the checking routine with your partner, if possible, but you both need to be consistent in your approach. Only try this when you are sure that your baby is not ill, hungry, or in any kind of discomfort.

You can encourage your baby to sleep in the following way:

● Adopt a "checking" routine—start by waiting for five minutes after she wakes up crying before going in to her.

When you leave the room, she will probably continue to cry, but wait for a minute longer than last time before going to check on her again.

● Each time you go in to check on her, keep the room dark, speak softly to her, stroke her, but don't pick her up. Firmly say good night and leave the room. It's important to stay calm—you will probably have to do this several times before your baby falls asleep.

● For babies who need you with them to settle down to sleep, try a gradual retreat, or "fading." Again, this works over several nights and involves your staying in the room with your baby until she falls asleep, but each night moving farther away from her crib. Eventually, you will be outside the room when she falls asleep.

How can I comfort my older baby?

There are many ways you can comfort your older baby. Toys and games are now a convenient source of amusement to share with her if she's crying for your attention, while diversions and distractions work well when tears of frustration are threatening. And, of course, there will still be times when only a loving hug will do.

New ways to comfort her

★ **Toys** Choosing toys that are suitable for her stage of development will entertain your baby best. This is not just to ensure that the toy is safe for her to use, but also to avoid frustration if it's beyond her capabilities. Once she can grasp, she'll love rattles or musical toys. When she sits up, stacking cups and shape sorters will be fun. As soon as she's mobile, she'll enjoy anything she can push or pull. And closer to her first birthday, she'll be ready for simple puzzles.

★ **Laughter** Using humor will often avoid tears. Singing a song, such as "This is the way we wash our hands," can amuse your baby when routine tasks need to be done.

CUDDLE UP
You're still your baby's best comforter. She doesn't want to be apart from you at the moment, and a hug from you can make everything better, helping her feel secure and loved, and allaying her fears.

★ **Action rhymes** Songs and rhymes with actions that you and your child can learn together, such as "Humpty Dumpty," "Patty-Cake," or "The Wheels on the Bus," can be energetic and great fun. Games that lead to a tickle, a hug, and shared laughter, such as "This Little Piggy," will soon become familiar to her and have her giggling in anticipation of the ending.

★ **Distractions and diversions** If you see trouble brewing, quickly try to turn your baby's attention to a new toy, or something that may be happening outside: "Oh listen, I think I can hear Daddy coming" or "Can you see a bird in the tree?" If she's playing with something you'd prefer she didn't have, offer her an interesting alternative rather than simply taking it away.

MAKE MUSIC TOGETHER
Musical instruments are not just for singing along to. Your baby will learn "cause and effect"—that by banging, shaking, or blowing, she can make a sound happen. Even some pans and a wooden spoon will do—if you can stand the noise!

SHARE A BOOK
It's never too soon to introduce your baby to books. She'll enjoy hearing you tell the story again and again and will point out familiar objects in the colorful pictures. Books that have different textures for her to feel and lift-the-flap stories add to her interest.

" Sonny's been so much **more settled** over the past few weeks— sometimes he'll go for five hours without waking. I love watching him as he sleeps. He looks like **an angel**. "

HANNAH, mother of
six-month-old Sonny

Sleep routines

By the time your baby is six months old, his world will be an endless source of fascination, and he will be wide awake and alert during play periods. While he's more likely to sleep well after these interludes of intense activity, he may be less willing to cooperate at naptimes or bedtime—after all, there are so many interesting things to do! This is when you will reap the rewards of having daytime and bedtime routines.

Longer nights

From six months, your baby will be able to sleep for longer periods at night. He'll probably spend around 11 hours asleep at night, although this is unlikely to be all in one uninterrupted stretch.

At this stage, most babies also take two regular daytime naps of an hour or more (one in the morning and one in the afternoon), but patterns will vary considerably.

Although many babies settle nicely into a healthy sleeping routine at this stage, many more will go through periods of disrupted night sleep.

Separation anxiety

At some point during the second half of his first year, your baby may suddenly start to become tense and fearful around strangers; he may cry when you leave the room or give him to someone else to hold (even someone familiar to him), and he may seem more clingy than usual. This is known as separation anxiety, and it is an important step forward in your baby's emotional development.

Separation anxiety is a healthy indication that your baby is slowly becoming aware of his independence from you, which is both exciting and frightening for him.

Your baby may suddenly become difficult to settle down. He may get upset when you leave him to go to sleep, and bedtime and nighttime awakenings may suddenly become complicated by problems that up until now hadn't bothered him. He may also be uncharacteristically frightened by loud noises or changes in routine, and he may start to wake up at night and cry for you.

Checklist

There are several new reasons for night waking in babies from around six months of age.

- Your baby reaches many important developmental milestones during this period, and this may temporarily disrupt his sleep, particularly when he is acquiring his gross motor skills.

- Some connection between sleeping and eating remains, but the link is not as strong as it was. He no longer needs to feed at night, for example, so night feedings should be curtailed with your help (see page 114).

- Any changes in your baby's routine—for example, new childcare arrangements, illness, or moving—may temporarily disrupt sleep.

- Your baby now has a growing sense of being an individual, and may wake up and miss you in the night.

- He's now able to stay awake at will.

This is a normal and temporary phase, so stick to your routines as much as possible. Be extra loving and attentive toward your baby during the day, and keep nighttime interactions with him supportive and caring, but brief and matter-of-fact.

It may be tempting to take him into bed with you as he goes through this phase, but you could be storing up trouble if you expect him to sleep in his own bed afterward. Although you may have to go into his room more frequently during this period to reassure him with calming words or a gentle stroke, at other times he may settle down if you simply call out to let him know you are near. A comforting or "transitional" object (see page 118) may help him now.

GETTING HER BACK TO SLEEP
Keep nighttime interactions with your baby brief. Speak softly to her, perhaps stroke her hand, but don't pick her up.

Any changes in your baby's daily routine may lead to a period of increased waking during the night. One significant change that could happen around this time is your return to work. As well as missing you, your baby will be coping with a new childcare arrangement. If he goes to daycare, he may have to adapt to a new nap routine and the extra stimulation of a busy environment.

You may want to keep your baby up for a while when you come home from work. You can prepare for this before you return to work by moving his bedtime back gradually. But again, stick to his usual routine, and a bedtime of no later than 8:30 pm.

Avoiding overtiredness

Until now, there wasn't much to keep your baby up at night. But with so many new discoveries to make, toys

Giving up night feedings

From around six months, your baby no longer needs to be fed during the night. He may give up his night feedings himself, but it's more likely that he will need your help. The best way of doing this is to progressively reduce the amount of milk he has during night feedings. Stopping suddenly is not advisable—although your baby wouldn't suffer nutritionally, he has learned to wake up expecting to be fed. You need to retrain him so that he no longer associates waking up or falling asleep with feeding. The following is only a suggestion, but it is one that has worked for many parents.

● **If you are breastfeeding,** you can judge how much milk your baby is getting by the number of minutes he spends at the breast. Reduce this by a minute each night, and increase the periods between feedings by half an hour.

● **If bottle-feeding,** put 1 fl oz (30ml) less in the bottle for nighttime feedings. Decrease by the same amount every night; increase the time between feedings by half an hour.

● **When your baby wakes up** and it's not time for a feeding, comfort him, but don't hold him. Pat him or speak to him softly, then leave the room once he is calm.

● **Enlist the help of your partner.** If you are breastfeeding, your partner may have more success in settling your baby than you because your baby won't be agitated by the smell of your milk.

It may take several days, but if you persevere, your baby will learn that his night wakings will not be rewarded with a feeding and should sleep through as a result.

to play with, and physical skills to perfect, your baby may not want to take time out to sleep.

Because his brain no longer simply "shuts down" when he's tired, he is able to stay awake even when he needs to sleep. Missing naps or going to bed late will make him irritable and may stop him from settling down and make him more likely to wake up during the night.

So, to keep your baby from getting overtired, be consistent in your approach to his daytime naps and bedtime routines. Even if he doesn't seem tired, go through his usual calming bedtime rituals with him. Don't wait until he seems really tired before trying to settle him in— putting him to bed calm and in a good mood is far more effective than if he's agitated and tearful.

Questions & Answers

My nine-month-old baby has suddenly stopped taking his morning nap. Is one daytime nap enough for him?

Many babies give up one of their naps as they reach their first birthday, although others may continue to nap twice a day well into their second year. You'll know whether one nap a day is enough by your baby's mood. If he's irritable and overtired by lunchtime, it may be that he needs extra sleep but is fighting it because he's too excited by what's going on around him. Try putting him down right after lunch. He will probably take a longer nap than usual—perhaps around two hours— and this may become his only nap of the day.

CHECKING ON YOUR BABY
If you want to make sure your baby is sleeping soundly during the night, always try to do so from the door of his room to avoid disturbing him if he's in a light stage of sleep.

❝ Often, Callum cries for me to stay as he falls asleep. To break the habit, each night I move farther from his crib until I'm outside, and out of sight! ❞

EVE, mother of 9-month-old Callum

What is a good bedtime routine for my nine-month-old?

The benefits of having a well-established bedtime routine in place for your baby at this stage cannot be overemphasized. If you're not sure what to include in your baby's bedtime routine, try some of the suggestions here. Experiment and see what works best for you and your baby.

Bedtime routines

A regular bedtime routine will:

★ give her the signals she needs that the day is over and that it's time to wind down and go to sleep

★ help promote healthy and peaceful sleeping habits

★ give your baby a real sense of security

★ become an enjoyable and fulfilling part of your relationship for many years to come

★ help you settle your baby down after there's been some kind of disruption in her life, such as illness or a move, or perhaps when staying away from home.

From now on, it's a good idea to feed your baby before you begin her bedtime routine. This will help

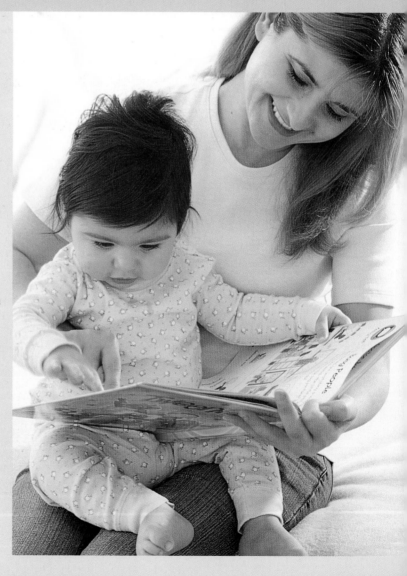

IT'S STORYTIME
Reading together is the perfect opportunity for a cuddle before bedtime, as well as encouraging your baby's love of books.

her to disassociate sleeping from feeding, and it means she won't fall asleep at the breast or bottle. Learning to go to sleep without you is an invaluable skill. You could try some or all of the following in your baby's bedtime routine:

★ **Give her a bath** A bath is not just a way to keep your baby clean—it is warming and relaxing.

★ **Brush her teeth** Remember to do this every night after her last feeding.

★ **Dim the lights** When it's time to put on her pajamas or sleeper, draw the curtains in her bedroom, dim the lights, and keep noise levels low. Any distractions should be kept to a minimum.

★ **Tell her a story** Settle down together and spend some quiet time looking at a book. Read to her, look at the pictures, and let her explore the book and turn the pages if she wants to.

★ **Give her a cuddle** A good-night kiss and cuddle before you lift her into her crib will be a pleasurable end to the day for you both. Place your baby's favorite soft toy or blanket in her bed to help comfort her.

★ **Say good night** Once your baby is settled in, leave the room. If she stirs or cries, wait a few minutes to see if she quiets down again. If she doesn't, go back in, say good night again, and leave.

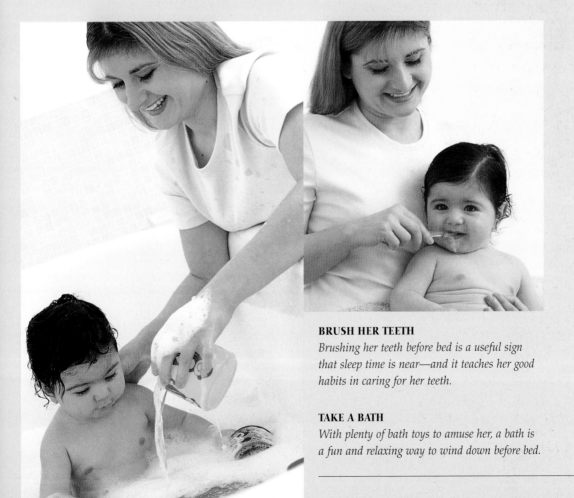

BRUSH HER TEETH
Brushing her teeth before bed is a useful sign that sleep time is near—and it teaches her good habits in caring for her teeth.

TAKE A BATH
With plenty of bath toys to amuse her, a bath is a fun and relaxing way to wind down before bed.

Getting ready for bed

Once you have established your baby's bedtime routine, it's worth building in some time beforehand to allow him to wind down from the day's activities.

It's a good idea to avoid boisterous activities and watching television in the hour or so before bedtime. Choose something soothing instead, such as looking at a book together. Other ways to ensure that your baby is ready for bedtime include:

• avoiding giving him a heavy meal or a lot to drink before bedtime; a light snack or small drink is plenty

• not letting him fall asleep over his last feeding, so you can put him to bed awake but sleepy

• never leaving your baby with a bottle in his bed, since this can cause ear infections and tooth decay

• once you've put him down, refraining from rushing in to him at the first sound you hear, unless he really is in distress—if you leave him for a few minutes, he may settle down on his own.

Comfort objects

Between the ages of eight and 15 months, your baby may become attached to a certain object, such as a cuddly blanket or soft toy. These comforters are known as "transitional objects" and can help smooth the emotional passage from dependence to independence,

" Ella won't go to sleep without her special blanket. She takes it with her to bed, and always looks for it during the day when she's tired or feeling unsure. I'm glad that she finds it such a comfort. "

CLAIRE, mother of nine-month-old Ella

especially when your baby is going through the developmental phase known as separation anxiety (see page 105). Having a comforting, familiar transitional object to snuggle up with or cling to:

• reassures your baby when he's away from you

• helps him feel at home whenever he's in a strange place

• calms him down whenever he's feeling upset

• helps him relax into sleep.

Many parents find these comfort objects very helpful and actively encourage such an attachment, so that the chosen object becomes an indispensable companion for their child. You may want to keep a duplicate so that you can wash and dry one while the other is in use, and to be sure that you always have a replacement if the precious original is ever lost.

You will find that your baby will gradually give up his comfort object on his own as he finds more mature ways to deal with life's challenges.

For some babies, a pacifier is a transitional object, but it's advisable to wean your baby off a pacifier before he comes to rely on it as a part of his comforting routine. Pacifiers at this stage can interfere with the development of your baby's language skills, may lead to more disturbed nights, and can be a difficult habit to break in later years (see page 59).

Questions & Answers

My seven-month-old bangs his head against the crib as he goes to sleep. Is this normal?
From around six months or so, a small percentage of babies and young children develop a habit of banging their heads against their crib bars or mattress, or indulge in some other repetitious, rhythmic activity, such as rocking themselves to sleep. While it may look alarming, this is not usually a sign that anything is wrong. It may last weeks, months, or even years, but should stop by age three. If your baby is happy and isn't bruising himself, don't worry. But if head-banging takes up a lot of his time, or if he displays other unusual behavior or is developing slowly, see your healthcare provider.

Coping with teething

Teething is often blamed for night waking, but in many cases this is a false diagnosis. Your baby's first teeth will appear between 5 and 10 months, and this coincides with the onset of waking for other developmental reasons.

Symptoms of teething include mild irritability and drooling. The gums around the emerging teeth may be swollen and tender, and he may want to bite on something firm, such as a teething ring, his fist, or your finger. Talk to your healthcare provider if your baby is clearly uncomfortable.

It's important not to blame teething every time your baby seems unsettled—he could be ill. A slightly raised temperature is normal when teething, but a temperature of 100.4°F (38°C) or more will not be caused by teething, nor will diarrhea or vomiting. In these cases, see your healthcare provider.

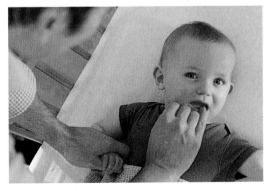

MAKING IT BETTER
Gently massaging your teething baby's gums with your fingertip can help soothe his discomfort.

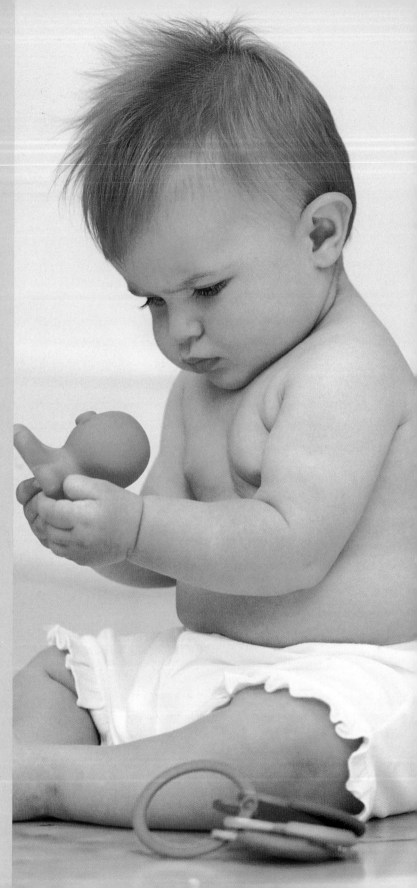

" Phoebe's always putting things in her mouth, especially **her toys**. I do wash them from time to time, but I also check for **broken parts** and throw the toys away if I find any. "

KATE, mother of six-month-old Phoebe

Your baby's safety

Whether your child has just learned to roll over or climb his first tree, each milestone brings feelings of pride and fulfilment to both of you. However, every new skill your child masters brings with it its own set of safety rules. So, throughout his early childhood, you will need to be one step ahead of him to keep him safe.

The first (and easiest) thing you can do to safeguard your child is simply to look around your home. Sit on the floor for a child's-eye view, and think about the things that are likely to attract his natural curiosity.

As your child grows, continue to see things from his perspective, and reevaluate safety requirements. At the same time, teach him to become more aware of potential dangers, by explaining in simple terms which things can burn or hurt, for example.

Childproofing your home doesn't have to be complicated. Simply removing sharp items from floor-level cupboards in your kitchen, installing safety locks and electrical outlet covers, and securing any unsteady furniture means you are childproofing. Whatever measures you take, they should help make you—and your child—feel safer and more relaxed.

Fire safety

Fires are the biggest single cause of accidental death of children in the home, and are mostly the result of smoke inhalation. Following the recommended safety rules will significantly reduce the risk of a fire in your home—and may save lives.

- Install smoke alarms.
- Don't smoke in your house. If you must, make sure cigarettes and matches are extinguished completely, and dispose of them safely. Keep matches and lighters out of your child's reach.
- Work out an escape plan for you and your family. Get advice from your local fire department.
- As soon as your child is old enough, tell him what to do if he discovers a fire or hears the alarm.
- Keep all doors shut at night.
- Keep a fire extinguisher in your kitchen. A fire blanket is handy, too.
- Replace old or worn electrical cords and don't overload electrical outlets.

Expert tips

Infants, toddlers, and preschool children should never be given toys with any of the following:

- electrical parts—anything that needs plugging in

- parts that could be pulled off and swallowed and/or fit into a child's nose or ear

- exposed wires and parts that can get hot

- lead paint or other toxic materials (use nontoxic paints and crayons)

- breakable parts

- sharp points or edges

- glass or thin parts

- springs or hinges that can pinch tiny fingers or get caught in hair.

Dealing with burns and scalds

Between the ages of six months and two years, your child is more likely to burn or scald himself than at any other time in his life. Acting fast can make a burn much less serious than it might otherwise be.

What to do

• No matter how small or large the burn, immediately flood the affected area with cold running water for at least 10 minutes. Keep the rest of your child's body warm.

• If clothes are not stuck to your child's skin around the burned area, remove them (cut them, if need be) but if anything is sticking to the burn, do not attempt to remove it.

• If the burn is large or severe or you are at all concerned, **call 911**.

• Cover the area with a sterile dressing or any lint-free material to keep out infection. Plastic wrap can make a good temporary covering if nothing else is available. Never apply creams or lotions to the skin.

• Large burns should always be seen by a doctor, but even smaller

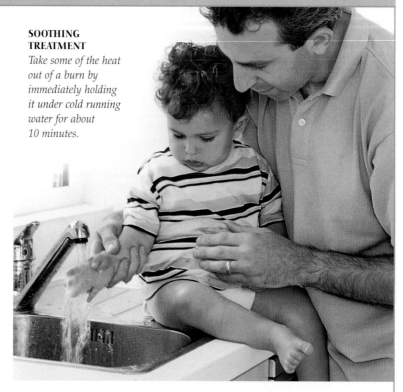

SOOTHING TREATMENT
Take some of the heat out of a burn by immediately holding it under cold running water for about 10 minutes.

burns may need medical attention, especially if the skin blisters. Don't break blisters—this can cause infection.

• If your child's clothes catch fire, drop him to the floor and roll him in a coat, blanket, or rug. Don't try to remove his

clothes. Follow the first aid advice above and **call 911**. If the fire is electrical, switch off electricity at the main circuit before applying first aid.

• Hold chemical burns under cold water for 20 minutes and **call 911**.

• If a fire starts in your home, shut the door on it, leave the building immediately, and **call 911** from a neighbor's house or a cell phone.

Fireplaces and heaters

Any fire with an open flame should have a protective firescreen around it.

• Never leave your child unattended in a room with a burning fire, even if it has a firescreen.

• Don't place anything on the screen.

• Keep all furniture at least 3 ft (1 m) away from an open fire.

• Never let your child see you throwing things onto the fire.

• Keep temperatures down on hot-water radiators to avoid burns, and teach your child that they are hot and must never be touched.

• If you use space heaters, keep your child and any furniture well away from them. Never place a heater on any surface but the floor.

Kitchen safety

For a small child, the kitchen is the most dangerous place in the house. Ideally, you should keep your baby or child out of the kitchen at all times, but often this isn't practical. Try at least to keep him out when you are cooking. Installing a safety gate at the kitchen door will help.

Cabinets and drawers

● Use safety latches to keep cabinets, drawers, and doors off-limits to your child.

● Store cleaners, bleach, furniture polish, dishwasher detergent, and other dangerous products in a high cabinet, preferably lockable, out of sight. These substances are lethal and should never be left within reach.

● If you have no option but to store some items under the sink, buy safety locks that latch automatically every time you close the doors.

● Never transfer toxic substances into containers that look as though they might hold food or drinks.

● Keep knives, forks, scissors, and other sharp instruments away from safer kitchen utensils, and in a latched drawer.

● Store plastic bags in a drawer or cabinet with a safety latch.

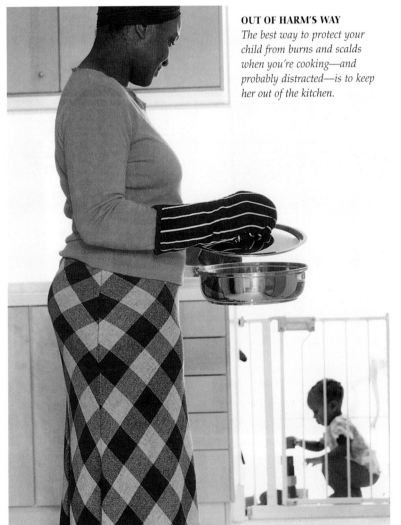

OUT OF HARM'S WAY
The best way to protect your child from burns and scalds when you're cooking—and probably distracted—is to keep her out of the kitchen.

Expert tips

The stove is potentially the most dangerous kitchen appliance.

● Always turn pot and pan handles toward the back of the stove.

● Whenever you're cooking or carrying hot food, keep your child out of the kitchen so you don't trip over him—a safety gate across the kitchen doorway is a good idea.

● When cooking, try to use the back burners only.

● If you have a gas stove, turn the dials firmly to the "off" position, and, if they're easy to remove or cover, do so when you are not cooking.

● Install a stove or oven guard.

● Teach your child that the oven is hot and not for touching, and keep reinforcing this message.

Aluminum foil and plastic-wrap boxes can also be hazardous, since their serrated edges can cut little fingers.

• Unplug appliances on counters when not in use, and keep cords out of your child's reach.

Household appliances

Refrigerators, freezers, washing machines, and dryers could be lethal if your child becomes trapped in one by climbing inside. If the door closes on them, tight-fitting seals will cut off the air supply, and a child's cries may go unheard. Warn your child of the dangers of playing inside an appliance, and keep all doors firmly closed after use. When discarding appliances, remove the doors first. Some other safety tips concerning household appliances include:

Garbage cans

Garbage cans often look inviting to young children, who enjoy nothing more than pawing through the contents for interesting playthings.

• Keep garbage cans locked in a cabinet or in the garage, if possible.

• When disposing of broken glass, always wrap it well in newspaper before placing it in the garbage.

• Tie knots in plastic bags before throwing them away.

CUPBOARD LOCKS
Some safety locks fit inside closet and cabinet doors, allowing you to open them a little way before releasing the catch. These safety latches automatically lock as you close the door.

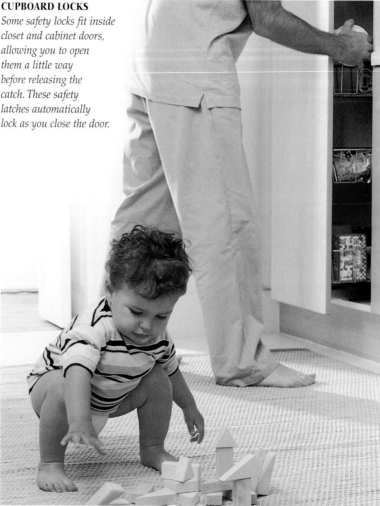

• Keep your microwave unplugged when it's not in use.

• Never use the microwave to warm baby bottles or food, since it heats things unevenly, leaving hot pockets that can scald your child's mouth.

• Always make sure that your dishwasher door is securely closed, unless you are loading or unloading the dishes. When the door is open, keep your child out of the way. Not only is this a dangerous tripping hazard—he may also be tempted to stand or sit on the open door, and an unanchored machine may tip over.

• When loading the dishwasher, always place cutlery in the appropriate tray, handle-side up, so that no sharp points or edges face upward when the door is open.

Stair gates

Once your child starts to crawl—and preferably beforehand—it's best to install stair gates at the top and bottom of your stairway.

● There are many types of stair gates on the market; if you are choosing one for the top of a staircase, make sure that it screws into the wall for extra strength. Stair gates that use pressure or suction are not recommended for use at the top of the stairs, since your child could push through them and fall. Accordion-style gates, which can trap arms or even necks, are also not recommended.

● Make sure the space between the stair gate and the floor is less than 2 in (5 cm) wide.

● Leave the first two or three stairs at the bottom of your staircase open, so that your baby can practice climbing on them.

Windows

Falls make up a large proportion of injuries in children under five. The majority of these are from windows, furniture, stairs, and playground equipment.

For this reason, avoid putting any furniture under windows, where it will tempt little climbers, and make sure there are window guards on all windows. This will go a long way toward giving you peace of mind. Make sure, however, that you can open all windows in case of fire. Keep keys nearby but out of your child's reach—you could even tape them to the upper frame.

The majority of falls from windows happen during spring and summer, when windows are more likely to be left open. If you need to open your windows, do so from the top instead of the bottom. If this is not possible, install safety guards, which you should have in any case, and make sure they cannot be opened, except by an adult or an older child, in the event of an emergency.

Be sure to tie all curtain and blind cords onto wall brackets in order to keep them out of a child's reach; cords with loops should be cut to prevent accidental strangulation.

Staying safe on the stairs

Thousands of children under the age of five are injured falling down stairs every year.

● As soon as your child is able to climb up and down stairs, spend the time to teach him how to get up and down safely. Young children (under the age of two and a half) might find it easier to crawl upstairs rather than walk, and climb downstairs backward, as if coming down a ladder.

● Never let your child climb up or down stairs unsupervised until you are absolutely sure of his competence.

● Make sure all handrails are sturdy, with less than 4 in (10 cm) between balusters or posts. If these spaces are any wider, your baby or child could get his neck or head caught between them. Staircases with wide gaps should be boarded up.

● Staircases should have no horizontal bars or slats—your child

Questions & Answers

How can I prevent my child from getting an electric shock? The most effective step you can take is to install plastic outlet covers on all outlets that are not being used. It's also a good idea to get into the habit of unplugging appliances when not in use and putting on outlet covers.

Children may be tempted to chew on power cables, as well as tug them, and this can also be a cause of electrocution. Use cord shorteners to tie up loose wires, and make sure cable is always held in place behind heavy furniture. Alternatively, staple or tape it to the floor or walls.

Check electric cords frequently and replace any worn ones. Never run cables or cords under carpets or rugs.

A well-stocked medicine and first aid cabinet is essential, but it must be locked and kept out of reach of children.

- Keep all medications locked up, and make sure their containers are shatterproof and have safety caps.

- Don't keep leftover prescription medicine after the end of a course of treatment. Flush it down the toilet.

- Never tell your child that medicine tastes good or that it's "like candy."

- Store vitamins in a safe place too, since children can overdose on them.

- If your child does swallow medicine, or any poison of any kind, get whatever you can out of his mouth and **call 911 immediately**. Have the bottle in your hand so that you can tell the emergency operator what was ingested and roughly how much. Do not give your child anything to eat or drink unless the emergency operator tells you to do so.

THE MEDICINE CABINET
Your medicine cabinet should be positioned well out of reach of your child. Medicines and other dangerous items should be kept locked up at all times.

may use them as a ladder. If need be, remove them or board them up.
- Keep stairs clutter-free. If you are in the habit of leaving things on the stairs to take on the next trip, place a sturdy box in the hallway to accommodate these items.
- Leave a night-light on in the hallway for older children who need to get up in the night.

Bathroom safety

The simplest way to avoid bathroom injuries is to make this room inaccessible unless your child is with an adult. This may mean installing a latch or lock on the outside of the door at adult height.

A child can drown in as little as 2 in (5 cm) of water, so it is not only the bathtub that poses a threat: Toilet bowls, diaper pails, and sinks, for example, can be just as dangerous. There are other potential hazards to try to avoid as well.
- Keep toothpaste, mouthwashes, soaps, and shampoos high up or in a cabinet with a safety latch or lock. Sharp objects such as razor blades, scissors, and nail clippers should also be locked up.

NONSLIP TUB
A nonslip bath mat or adhesive strips will protect your child from nasty bumps when he's in the tub.

Water temperature

Injuries caused by scalding bath water often involve large parts of the body and require hospitalization and skin grafts. This is why it is important that you run the cold water into the bathtub before adding the hot water, and always test the temperature before letting your child get in. Also remember that a child can bump into a hot faucet and sustain a serious burn. One of the most effective ways to prevent burns and scalds is to turn your water-heater thermostat down. Safety experts recommend that hot water should come out of faucets at no more than 120°F (49°C).

• Remove all electrical items, such as hair dryers, razors, and radios, from the bathroom.

• Never throw used razor blades, toothbrushes, or other potentially dangerous materials into the bathroom wastebasket.

• Make sure that shower doors or other surfaces are made of safety glass or shatterproof material.

• Throw away soap when it is small enough to fit inside your child's mouth. Children can choke on soap.

• Many accidents occur while a caregiver leaves a baby or toddler unattended "just for a minute" to answer the telephone. Take your child with you, get a cordless telephone, use a cell phone, or switch on the answering machine.

In the bathtub

Never, *under any circumstances*, leave your baby or child unsupervised in the bathtub. Children can drown in seconds. If you have to go to the door or phone, take your child out of the bath, wrap him in a towel, and take him with you when you go to answer it.

Remember that bath seats and rings designed for young babies are meant to be bathing aids, not safety aids. They will not keep your child from drowning while unattended.

There are also other important bathtime safety considerations:

• Place a nonslip mat or strips on the bottom of your bathtub.

• Always run the cold water before the hot, and then mix the water so

that it feels just warm. Test it with your inner wrist or elbow before putting your baby in the water.

• Always use both hands to lift your baby into and out of the tub.

• Cover faucets with washcloths during bathtime.

Toilets

• Get into the habit of keeping the toilet lid down at all times—use a toilet lock if you want to be particularly careful.

• Never leave toilet cleaner in the toilet bowl to soak. Use it and then flush it away.

9-12 months

"In the space of **just a year** he really has developed into his own little person."

DEE, mother of 12-month-old Cameron

" Feeding Nicole is **much simpler** now. I take some potatoes, vegetables, and meat out of our main meal and mash it up for her. It's **better than ready-made** any day. "

CAROLINE, mother of nine-month-old Nicole

Feeding your older baby

Your baby's personality is starting to shine through, and as her sense of self grows, so does her desire for independence. Over the next few months, she'll work hard at learning how to feed herself, and with your patience and praise, she'll soon master this essential skill. Meanwhile, you can enjoy her company at the table—this is a great time to start letting her join in on family meals.

Advancing skills

Your baby now has regular mealtimes with three meals—breakfast, lunch, and dinner—every day and two or three snacks as well. She can cope well with mashed or chopped food and uses finger foods to practice her chewing skills. There is now little she can't eat, so family meals can be easily adapted to feed your baby, too. Keep talking to her about what you are doing when you are preparing the meals and give her lots of praise.

Your baby's new skills make mealtimes easier:
- she can now chew, cope with different textures, and pick up shapes (talk to your healthcare provider if she has difficulties with any of these)
- her hand–eye coordination is developing fast, and learning how to feed herself is a natural step toward independence

- she's starting to recognize lots of familiar words such as "cup" and "lunchtime"
- she loves interacting with people and will enjoy social get-togethers such as mealtimes.

Introducing new tastes

Your older baby is becoming much more active—learning to crawl and then walk—which means she needs extra calories for energy and growth. She also needs a wide variety of nutrients in her diet, so now is a good time to introduce her to a broader range of foods. Since her natural inclination is to explore everything she can get her hands on, including food, this is a great age to offer your baby new tastes, although as she enjoys some independence, she is also beginning to show clear food preferences.

Extra equipment

You will find the following items useful as your baby becomes more experienced at feeding herself:

- **plastic feeding bowl** with a suction pad to keep her from throwing food all over the floor

- **plastic bib** with a molded tray to catch the food that doesn't make it into her mouth

- **portable high chair** that screws or clips onto a tabletop—a great help when you are out visiting friends or relatives or on vacation.

Encouraging self-feeding

Your baby is developing a strong sense of her place in the family and of her daily routines. She'll start to look forward to mealtimes, and will recognize the cues that mean food is on the way. She'll also want to be just like you—which means feeding herself, rather than being fed by you. Encouraging your baby to self-feed means that, for a while at least, mealtimes will take longer and be messier. At first, your baby will probably keep turning over the spoon before it reaches her mouth. But as her finger and hand skills develop, she'll soon master the art of feeding herself.

Help her reach this milestone by:
- giving her lots of chances to practice—and ignoring the mess
- making sure she's getting enough food in her mouth by helping her load her spoon and slipping in mouthfuls with your own spoon between attempts
- serving her food that will stay on the spoon more easily—mashed potatoes with cheese, thick yogurts, and cottage cheese, for example
- resisting the temptation to take over—letting her struggle and succeed will boost her confidence.

Talk to your healthcare provider if your child shows no interest in self-feeding.

Getting the portions right

Every baby's appetite is different—and can change from day to day. This means it can be hard to judge how much food your baby needs. Remember that a baby's stomach can't hold very much and therefore she'll need to eat more frequently than you.

It's good to encourage your baby to eat at regular times, but accept also that she will probably need a snack between mealtimes to help fill the gaps. When she's uninterested, let her out of her high chair after 10 minutes or so and offer her another meal or snack a couple of hours later.

Teething and eating

When your baby is teething, don't be surprised if she loses her appetite. Over the next couple of months, she'll have lots of teeth coming in, and although some babies take teething in stride and show no ill effects, others become fretful and irritable.

The common signs of teething include swollen, reddened gums, excessive drooling, an inflamed cheek, a mild cough, and even a low-grade fever. Your baby will also want to bite down on anything she can get in her mouth.

If pain and discomfort affect your baby's appetite, she'll need more milk for a while. She may also refuse to drink from a cup, despite having previously loved the independence it gave her. Bottle-feeding your baby again shouldn't be a problem as long as it's only short-term.

Meanwhile, chewing and sucking on firm-textured finger food that becomes soft for easy swallowing can help soothe your baby's gums—and offer her some extra nutrition at the same time. You could try giving her a frozen banana, for example. But never leave her alone with food in case she chokes. Commercially made teething biscuits are best avoided, since they contain a lot of sugar. Cold food—such as chilled puréed apple—may also be more appealing than warm food.

**INDEPENDENT
FEEDING**

*The time will come
when your baby
wants her
independence.
Allowing her to feed
herself will boost her
confidence, and she
will quickly master
the skills she needs.*

Don't let your child carry a bottle or food around between meals or snacks (this will lessen her appetite), and a family rule of no food between meals will increase the likelihood of her eating more at mealtimes.

Planning her meals

Your baby should have at least one daily portion of fish, meat, eggs, lentils, or beans (these are the best sources of protein and iron), as well as food from the four main food groups every day. These groups are:

● dairy products, such as cheese, yogurt, or full-fat cottage cheese (don't rely on just cheese for protein; use meat, fish, or egg yolks, too)

● starchy foods, such as potatoes, bread, noodles, rice, pasta, and breakfast cereals

● fruits and vegetables: offer a selection of fresh fruits and vegetables so she gets used to different tastes and textures

Expert tip

Your baby can now eat the same food as you, as long as it doesn't contain added salt, sugar, or honey. You should also avoid giving her:

● foods that carry a high risk of food poisoning (such as mold-ripened cheese, liver pâté, and soft-boiled eggs)

● whole nuts (ground nuts are fine, unless there is a history of allergies, in which case you should avoid all nuts).

When can my baby join in family meals?

Now is a great time for your baby to join in with family meals. She's a little individual with a real personality, and she enjoys having fun with everyone. Her ability to understand language is growing, and she's really trying to communicate with you. Even if she doesn't have the same food, feeding your baby when the rest of the family is eating together has lots of benefits.

A FAMILY AFFAIR
Children who regularly eat meals with the family are less likely to be fussy eaters and more likely to try a wider range of foods.

It's good to eat together

Family mealtimes are about more than just making sure everyone is getting fed—they are also social occasions and great opportunities for your baby to learn about good table manners and conversation.

Eating with your baby will also make her more adventurous when it comes to food. A baby who won't eat green beans may change her mind when she sees everyone else enjoying them.

Keep the atmosphere light and easy-going by:

★ planning family meals around your baby—if she's tired, eating together won't be fun for you or her

★ not expecting too much—if your baby turns her nose up at the food on her plate, don't take it personally; there could be various explanations for why she's not hungry today

★ ignoring the mess—have lots of paper towels handy for cleaning up as she goes.

• meat (such as well-chopped chicken, lamb, or pork), soft flaked white fish, or small quantities of well-cooked lentils or beans.

Babies' appetites are very changeable, so check your child's diet over a week, not a day. Talk to your healthcare provider if you think your baby isn't eating all she needs for good nutrition.

Meal ideas

• Breakfast
Yogurt smoothie and toast; oatmeal with dried fruit; shredded wheat and milk with grated pears.

• Lunch
Lasagna; sausage, mashed potatoes, and vegetables; cut-up baked potatoes with hummus, avocado, or baked beans.

• Desserts
Baked bananas and full-fat plain yogurt, bread-and-butter pudding, whole-wheat pancakes with fresh fruit, canned fruit in natural juice.

Questions & Answers

My baby is now nine months old and she still has no teeth. Should I be worried about this?
Many babies at nine months are still toothless—and some make it to their first year without a tooth in sight. Late teething doesn't have to affect your baby's move to chunkier food. Babies with and without teeth use their gums for chewing until their molars appear in the middle of the second year.

My baby doesn't seem to eat very much. Should I be encouraging her to eat more?
Your baby's stomach will fill up quickly on solid food, so when she's had enough, don't insist she has one last mouthful. This may give her an aversion to the food she's eating as well as making her feel upset and resentful. Talk to your healthcare provider if your baby:
• tries to store food in her cheeks instead of swallowing it
• refuses to accept textured food.

Tips for healthy eating

One of the best ways you can help your baby to grow up fit and healthy is to help her develop healthy eating habits now. These guidelines will help:

● **If she rejects something today, try again a few days later.**
A baby's tastes are notoriously fickle, and just because she appears not to like something now, there's no reason to assume she won't enjoy it another time. It can take 10–20 tries before a baby accepts a new food, and sometimes even more.

● **Praise her when she eats well.**
Your baby will quickly realize that healthy, natural food is good for her if you tell her what a good girl she is when she eats it.

● **Avoid sugary treats.**
Sugar and sugary foods contain what is termed "empty calories"— lots of sugar and energy but little nutritional value.

● **Offer healthy snacks.**
It may be easier to reach for the cookie jar when your baby is hungry between meals, but it's worth getting her used to nutritious snacks.

● **Don't allow your child to graze between meals.**
If your child sits in her high chair for a meal or snack every two to three hours, she will not be hungry in between—don't allow her to carry food or drinks around with her.

Milk needs

Your baby should still be having at least 17–20 fl oz (500–600ml) of breast milk or formula a day (this is equivalent to about two breastfeeds). Around this age, however, she may start to wean herself off the breast.

Losing interest in sucking can happen if your baby is eating lots of solids and is good at using a cup. It may, however, only be temporary. Perhaps your baby is teething, in which case sucking can put pressure on painful gums. Your baby is also curious about the world around her—and she may be easily distracted if people are in the room or the television is on. Feed her in a quiet room without distractions.

Meanwhile, make sure your baby is getting her full milk quota by offering her formula in her cup. If she doesn't like this, supplement her diet with plenty of full-fat yogurt and hard cheese.

● **Avoid fast food.**
Pizza, chicken nuggets, and french fries are high in fat and salt and may contain additives. If your child eats these foods regularly, she may have a greater risk of developing health problems as an adult.

Thirst quenchers

Your baby may still be resisting using a cup, but it's worth persisting with this. Drinking from a cup is better for speech development and for her teeth.

Give your baby water between meals if she seems thirsty. During the summer, when she is losing fluid through sweat, you should also offer her a drink of water a couple of times during the day. Don't make a habit of giving her juice too often—4 fl oz (120ml) a day is plenty—because she'll love the sweeter taste and quickly refuse anything else. Too much fruit juice can cause diarrhea and diaper rash and contribute to poor dental health.

Flying food

Your baby is now much more skilled with her hands. She has mastered the pincer grasp and can pick up anything she comes across using her thumb and forefinger. This means she can guide pieces of food into her mouth more accurately—so self-feeding is getting much less messy.

She's also figured out how to "let go" of things. Be prepared for lots of dropping and picking up games (she drops, you pick up). By the end of her first year she'll have discovered how to throw, too.

" I always make extra for Rashmi and then freeze it for meals the following week. This saves me time—and also makes me feel less frustrated if she doesn't eat much. "

NAWSHEEN, mother of 11-month-old Rashmi

" I breastfed Sam for **one year** and it was a special time. When he stopped nursing, I felt a little sad, but mostly I was glad that we'd done it. I'll always know I gave him the **best start.** "

EMMA, mother of sixteen-month-old Sam

How long should I breastfeed?

Although the American Academy of Pediatrics (AAP) recommends breastfeeding for one year, the decision to stop or continue breastfeeding is up to you. Many babies who are exclusively breastfed, and who start drinking cow's milk after the first year, usually want to keep nursing. Others phase out breastfeeding gradually toward the end of their first year.

Changing preferences

If you have chosen to mix breast and bottle, you may find your baby starts to prefer her bottle as she nears the end of her first year. This is because the milk from a bottle flows more easily and quickly than the milk from a breast, and older babies tend to become more impatient if they know there's a faster option. By this stage you'll know that your baby has had huge benefits from being breastfed.

Giving fewer feedings

You'll probably find that you naturally start giving fewer feedings during the second half of the first year. As your baby acquires a taste for solid food, and gets used to sitting in her high chair and participating in family meals, she'll often prefer that to being nursed on your lap.

Some mothers feel that by this stage they're ready to stop breastfeeding. If you are in this position and don't feel your baby is nursing any less, or isn't cutting down her feedings as quickly as you'd like, try this step-by-step plan to faster weaning:

Step 1: Skip the lunchtime breastfeed and offer a drink from a cup instead.
Step 2: After a few days, skip the midmorning feeding and offer a drink of water instead.
Step 3: Skip the final evening feeding or cut out the morning one. You will then be left with occasional snacks, if your baby still has these, and one sizable night or morning feeding.
Step 4: Cut out occasional feedings by distracting your baby at times when she wants to come onto your lap for a feeding. Another person—ideally, your partner—can help by

Myths about giving up breastfeeding

When to stop breastfeeding is your decision. In particular, you don't have to stop when:

- your baby cuts her first tooth
- she bites you (just say "no" very firmly and move her away from the breast—she'll soon realize that biting means no access to your milk, and won't continue to bite)
- she starts on solid food
- she starts to feed herself.

playing with her when she really wants to breastfeed.
Step 5: Eliminate the final morning or evening breastfeeding by changing your routine at that time of the day. Again, a partner or another family member can help by acting as a

DISTRACTION TECHNIQUES
Reading a book with your babies allows them to feel close to you while also taking their minds off wanting to nurse.

Expert tip

A final breastfeeding can be a difficult moment for you. Far better, therefore, not to have a formal "final feeding." Simply cut down and down until your baby or toddler is hardly ever nursing at the breast. Then, when she does want the breast, just try to distract her, but don't refuse completely if you can see it means a lot to her. That way you'll probably find your final breastfeeding goes unnoticed, because you'll never know she won't come back for "a little more" one day.

distraction. If your baby has a security blanket or a special toy, this can be very useful as well. Try to introduce a new "treat" into the picture—maybe a cup of warm milk for bedtime, or reading a new book, or, if it's the morning feeding, make a big treat out of dad taking the baby for an early playtime.

Giving up breastfeeding

Ending breastfeeding is much easier for both you and your baby if you do it gradually. Give up quickly, and you'll be far more likely to suffer engorged breasts because your body hasn't been able to react fast enough to the fact that you've eliminated so many feedings. Take it slowly, and your body will adjust with you.

Weaning slowly is also more pleasant for your baby, who may hardly notice that her breastfeedings are becoming less frequent. If you wean her too quickly, she's likely to be confused and hurt by your rejection of her needs: Your breasts have represented her strongest security to date. Abruptly withdrawing them may make her anxious.

Breastfeeding an older baby or toddler

Toddlers don't "need" breast milk for health reasons in the way that younger babies do. However, there's still evidence that the immunological advantages of breast milk continue to be useful. Breastfeeding can also:

● comfort your child when she has a fall or hurts herself

● offer an occasional "safe haven" at a time when she's branching out and sometimes finds the world a little overwhelming

● continue to reinforce the special relationship she has with her mom.

If you and your toddler are happy to go on breastfeeding, that's fine. In many parts of the world, children are routinely breastfed until at least the age of three, and sometimes even until they begin school at five.

Do what's right for you

In most Western countries, however, weaning has been sped up, and it's uncommon to see babies of more than six months being breastfed. This adds to a general sense that once a baby is in the second half of her first year, she should be weaned—although, by contrast, it's very common to see older babies out in public with bottles.

You shouldn't have to put up with negativity and judgmental comments if you choose to breastfeed your older baby, but some mothers say they get a lot of criticism. In Norway, a country with far better breastfeeding rates than we have in North America, breastfeeding toddlers are a common sight.

Staying close to your child

You'll want to find new ways of being close to your child now that you're not breastfeeding. There may be some special time of day when you can cuddle up together—sharing a book can replace the intimacy of your nursing together. Remember that you won't "lose" the closeness you've built up through breastfeeding: On the contrary, you'll go on building on it throughout the rest of your life.

How does it feel to stop nursing?

Some women say they're relieved when they decide to stop breastfeeding because they feel it has become restrictive, and like the sense of freedom and of having their bodies back to themselves. It's good to move on and to know your child is getting older, but for many moms there's also a tinge of regret that this phase is over.

If you hope to have more children, you may like to look forward to breastfeeding again with a new baby in the years ahead. If this is likely to be your only or your final child, however, you may feel a sense of sadness that a chapter of your life is now closing, particularly if you have nursed several children.

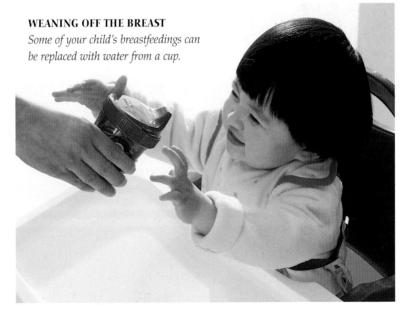

WEANING OFF THE BREAST
Some of your child's breastfeedings can be replaced with water from a cup.

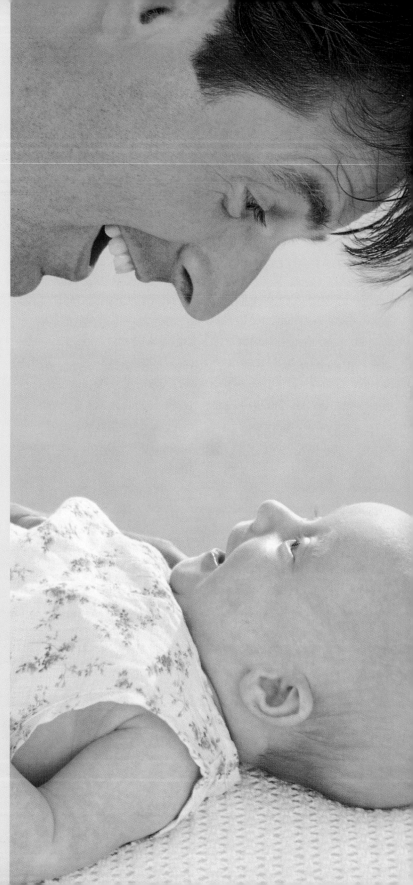

" Hannah started using her first words—she called our dog 'woof'— just before her **first birthday** but I had a strong sense that she had been building up to those **words for months.** "

JACK, father of 12-month-old Hannah

Learning to talk

From the moment your baby is born, and often before, you will notice his reactions to voices and other sounds. By the end of his first year, he will have become a collector of all the information he needs to produce his first words. The quest begins as soon as he is born because learning about the joys of human interaction has its roots in the first few weeks of life when you and your baby start getting to know each other.

The drive to communicate

From the moment he is born, your child is an active communicator. At first, his cries and burps relate only to how he is feeling, whether he is hungry, tired, needs a clean diaper, or has gas. Although he doesn't yet know that he is sending out a message, your response teaches him that his cries have consequences—they bring rewards. It's not long before he begins to use crying to express specific needs and focus it on the people who are likely to do something about them. He is already beginning to communicate.

Your first conversations are all about kindness, reassurance, and making him feel safe. Most parents chatter away to their babies without really being aware of it: "Hello, baby, did you wake up for your feeding?" "Over to Daddy, now—he wants to change your diaper." "Ooh, you don't want me to take off your T-shirt, do you?" To your baby, this is nothing more than a meaningless string of sounds, but they make him feel calm and attended to nonetheless.

Using all his senses

Your baby's rapid development in his first year involves all his senses—vision, hearing, touch, taste, and smell. As soon as he is born, they help him figure out who and what is important to him, and gradually, over the coming months, he learns to use his senses to gather information. Although he has always been able to hear, he must now learn to listen. As soon as he can focus, he begins learning to direct his attention so he can recognize gestures, facial expressions, familiar objects, and movements.

Checklist

Babies pass these talking milestones in their first year:

- cooing after six weeks
- babbling from six months; increasing experimentation with sounds
- beginning to use specific sounds in specific contexts—for example, "woof" for all animals
- by nine months, understanding "no" and "bye"
- by age one, recognizing some words and responding to requests such as "clap your hands"; possibly speaking one or two words.

The basics of talk

Most of the time we communicate so effortlessly, we fail to appreciate how complex human communication is. However, to understand how children learn to talk, it helps to separate out some of its different elements: these are communication, language, and speech.

Beginning to communicate

It seems that children are born not just to speak but also to interact with other people—first with their parents and soon afterward with everyone else around them. Long before your baby uses words, she uses cries and gestures to make her meaning clear, and learns to read and respond to the gestures and facial expressions of those who care for her.

At first, your interaction with your baby is made up of touching, rocking, smiling, and eye contact—gestures that convey your feelings more effectively than words can. They tell your baby that you love her and are interested in her. She understands emotion long before she can talk.

GESTURES
Smiles, touch, and eye contact tell your baby you are interested in who she is.

Gestures, facial expression, and body language are a major part of communication in these early months and continue to be so throughout life. Think how much you use them to enhance your speech and interpret what you hear. They are an essential fallback when a meaning is unclear or a language is foreign to you.

However, human communication is also about referring to and describing the world, and this is the next step your child takes toward becoming a talker. Once she has established what words do and how they relate to things, it is only a matter of time before she is naming what she sees— "doggy," "car," "milk," or "mom."

What is language?

Language in general, and grammar in particular, is what distinguishes humans from other animals. Our system of combining words into meaningful sequences enables us to give shape to our ideas and thoughts and convey them to others.

One of the really distinctive features of our capacity for language is our ability to be creative with sentences. Although we use some expressions over and over again, we are constantly producing new sentences that we have never said before and that we have never heard anyone else say either.

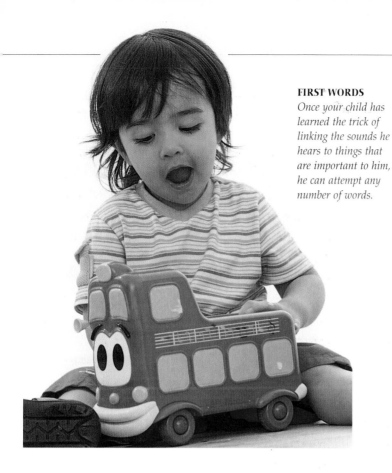

FIRST WORDS
Once your child has learned the trick of linking the sounds he hears to things that are important to him, he can attempt any number of words.

Checklist

Language is made up of:

● Phonemes such as /b/ and /p/—the smallest sound units of language. They are speech sounds, not letters, and there are about 40 in English.

● Morphemes—the smallest meaningful unit of language. "Do" is a morpheme, but so is "un-" because it changes or adds meaning.

● Syntax—the combination of words into phrases and sentences.

By two-and-a-half, most children are using the three main components of a complex language system. They learn the rules of *phonology* as they combine sounds into words. Then they come to grips with *syntax* as they combine words in the correct order to form phrases and sentences such as "Get ball" or "Juice all gone." Although these are simple requests and observations, they are *semantic* (they have a precise meaning). In fact, children start to put words together as soon as they want to communicate more complicated meanings.

Children's language skills are not simply confined to what they are able to say—they also need to understand what they hear. An essential part of learning to talk is using what they know about language to work out what others are saying.

Can other creatures talk?

Do any animals other than humans have language? Observers of animal communication have made some fascinating discoveries:

● The North American cicada has four different calls, each one with a different message. The vervet monkey has 36 calls.

● Bees dance in a pattern to direct other bees to nearby pollen supplies.

● Dolphins can communicate specific information to other dolphins.

● Mynah birds and parrots mimic speech, but there is no evidence that they can understand any of it.

● Chimpanzees and gorillas are the only animals with anything that resembles a human capacity for communication. They do not have the vocal apparatus for speech, but they can be taught to communicate using sign language, keyboards, and cards. In teaching programs, some have learned to use hundreds of signs and understand even more.

However, even the cleverest gorillas and chimpanzees are able to form only the most basic sentences. They do not come close to being as creative with language as the average two-year-old human being.

Finding her voice

Your baby's first sounds tend to be nasal because her voice box (larynx) is high up, close to her mouth, and her throat (pharynx) is short. She becomes able to make speech sounds as her larynx descends and her pharynx lengthens. This is happening rapidly by the end of her first year and is complete by age three.

Baby   Adult

Pharynx

Vocal fold

Larynx

Pharynx

Vocal fold

Larynx

Practicing her speech

Your baby's speech is made up of phonemes—all the sounds of the language or languages that she is learning in her first year, usually from her mom and dad. The earliest sounds she makes are not specific to any language, but by 12 months or so, she is already specializing in the ones she will need to use.

Making speech sounds is not an easy task for a baby and relies as much on her physical development as her growing ability to think. She has to be able to control her head, bring her lips together deliberately, move her tongue up and down, and use the soft palate at the top of her mouth to produce them. All of this has to be coordinated with her breathing and the movement of her voice box (larynx). At first, your baby will have little control over this, but by her first birthday she will be producing a range of sounds that are more and more like real speech. Soon she will be producing her first attempts at words.

SOUND PLAY
She loves to practice sounds, and uses them with all the variety and expression of real speech as she talks to her toys and "reads" from her books.

Critical time?

Do children have to learn language at a particular stage in their life? Is the chance lost forever if they are not given enough stimulation?

Since scientists cannot ethically prevent a child from learning language, answers to these questions have to be based on rare examples of children who have been raised in isolation, with no meaningful contact with humans. These studies indicate that a child who is not exposed to language in the first eight or nine years is very unlikely to learn it.

Although language learning is innate, it appears to rely on experiences during key periods for its development. The first six months of life seem to be critical for homing

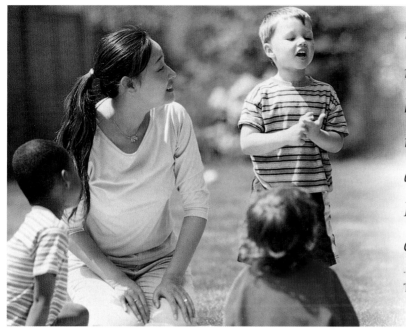

" It's incredible how rapidly Sam's speech has developed since those early babblings during his first year. His speech seems so confident now. "

TESS, mother of three-year-old Sam

in on the sounds of the child's native language, and in the years between one and five, grammar is more easily acquired than at any other time in life. There is also evidence that a child's early talking skills continue to have a bearing on the way the brain is configured once it becomes more specialized in language during adolescence.

What is certain is that the first three years of life are a critically important learning period for children. After the first year, language is the key that helps children unlock many of their discoveries about the world, enables them to order and express their thoughts and ideas, and opens the door to literacy.

Talking milestones

Babies acquire speech skills in the same order, whatever their language. These are the stages your baby passes through en route to becoming a talker:

● She makes nonverbal sounds and uses intonation to express what she wants. She points to ask for things or makes a noise to get attention.

● She uses her own versions of words that are understood within the family—for example, "ba-ba" becomes the family word for "banana." The rise and fall of her voice is still very important in letting you know what she means.

● She begins to use and speak her first conventional words.

● She uses single words to mean more than the thing she is referring to. For example, "drink" begins to mean "Can you get me a drink?"

● She uses two words together: "Mommy gone" or "More ball." Although she knows what she means, some phrases are not obvious to unfamiliar listeners and need to be deciphered by trial and error.

● She combines two or three words to make sentences that include an object or person (a noun) and something happening (a verb)— "Dog eat dinner."

● She links ideas using conjunctions such as "and" and uses word endings such as "-ed" to make different tenses.

How should I talk to my baby?

Babies become better talkers if they are spoken to a great deal by their parents and caregivers, but it's not simply a matter of the amount of speech they hear. There is a characteristic way in which most people talk to babies that helps them to focus on and absorb the sounds and words of a language. Experts call it "parentese."

What is parentese?

Do parents need to be instructed in parentese? Probably not at all. Just as your baby came into the world wired and ready to learn a language, your response to him seems to be programmed, too. You instinctively adjust your tone and style of language to suit his needs. Most grandparents do it quite naturally as well, and even young children seem to know that they have to change their speech when they are addressing babies and younger children. Here are the key features:

★ You speak in a higher-pitched voice and more slowly than normal, with clear pauses at the end of your sentences.

TIME FOR A TALK
The best time for a talk is when your baby is wide awake but not hungry and looks ready to play.

A FRIENDLY GREETING

Move in close when you start the conversation so he can focus on your face and meet your gaze. Start off the conversation with a broad smile and a question—"Hello, my beautiful Toby, are you all nice and clean now that you've had your bath?"

PAUSE AND WAIT

Now pause and wait. He may just look straight into your face with a big smile at first because it takes him a little while to work up his own response—perhaps a noise, a body movement, or a wave of the hands. If he is beginning to coo or babble, he may offer a string of sounds.

TIMING YOUR REPLY

Either copy his sounds or comment on them, "Oh, that was a good whoop." Don't wait too long before you reply—he may lose the connection between what you say and what he did, and the dialogue will be broken. Keep the conversation going until his interest begins to wane and he looks away.

★ You exaggerate your intonation, adopting a singsong voice that emphasizes important words.

★ Your sentences are short, simple, and grammatical, and also tend to be very repetitive.

★ You repeat back what your child has said or "recast" it to make it a little more complicated. Your baby says "shoe" and you respond with "Yes, you're putting on your shoe—it's a blue shoe."

★ Your vocabulary is "concrete" in that it tends to refer to people or things that are present, rather than ideas and things that cannot be seen.

The dance of interaction

First dialogues with your baby may only last a few minutes, but they contain some essential ingredients of conversation—good listening and turn-taking. So the next time you ask your baby a question that you assume will be rhetorical, wait for a moment and see if he has something to tell you in return (between two and seven seconds is the ideal pause). Not everyone gets the timing right at first, and babies are often thwarted in their first attempts at conversation. They get an enthusiastic welcome from a visitor, who then looks away to talk to someone else at the critical moment when they are just working up to waving their arms or offering an expressive grunt by way of a reply.

Babies love rituals that follow a set pattern and allow them to take control. When a conversation is working well, it is like a dance of interaction in which both partners know exactly what to expect.

Setting up little dialogues like this is a great way to let your baby know that he is being listened to and is important. He is being acknowledged as a conversational partner and learning that trying to communicate can pay off.

Your baby's name

The very first word that is likely to have meaning for your baby is his own name. He hears it whenever a familiar or new face says "hello" or "goodbye," and it occurs continually in the speech he hears from his parents and caregivers. Usually by the time he is four or five months old, he understands that his name has a special relevance to him, although it will be some time before he is able to say it himself.

Fine-tuning the sounds

Toward the end of his first year, your baby has a whole battery of sounds at his disposal, spoken with all the conviction and variety of real speech. He no longer tolerates being left out of conversations and can shout to get attention when he is ignored. Babies of this age really like to make their presence felt, especially when everyone else is silent. Solemn occasions in places of worship are a favorite time to exercise his voice— the echo is very rewarding.

LOOK, JAMES!
Now that he recognizes his own name, it is easier to initiate games and conversations and direct his attention to interesting sights and activities.

Your response to this sociable little person is changing, too. Now it seems positively rude not to address someone who is so obviously ready for conversational give and take.

● Make time to talk directly to your baby, particularly if life is becoming more hectic now that you are back at work. He needs face-to-face talk with lots of emphasis on key labeling words—"your cup," "Daddy's shoes"—rather than a sea of chatter.

● Even if you are not much given to emotional displays, emphasize your gestures and emotions when you talk to him—they give him vital clues to what you are saying.

● Try to understand his gestures and sounds. Follow his gaze and hazard a guess at what he might be labeling as a "bon." He will be thrilled if you hit on the correct thing. Repeat it back to him—"balloon"—and add some detail, but don't expect him to copy the word correctly.

Working up to words

Imagine your nine-month-old hears the following: "nowletsseewhatyouve beenuptoohdearyouhaveawetdiaper poorbabynowonderyouvebeencrying wedbetterchangeyou." To understand this stream of sounds, he has to listen carefully and learn to recognize where one word ends and another begins. "Now, let's see what you've been up

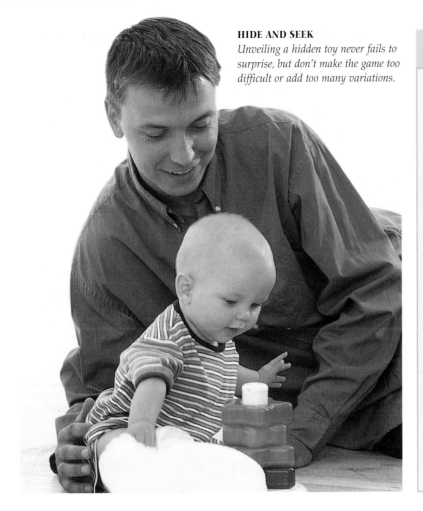

HIDE AND SEEK
Unveiling a hidden toy never fails to surprise, but don't make the game too difficult or add too many variations.

Expert tips

The best games for babies over six months are repetitive and predictable. It helps them to feel in control of events.

● Put a light scarf over your head and ask your baby to "find Mommy." Stay close so he can pull it off and reveal your face. Now drape it lightly over his head and ask "Where's Joey?" He will soon learn to pull it off himself.

● When your baby is 9 or 10 months old, cover up a toy within his reach, letting him watch you as you do it. Now ask him to find the toy. Look surprised and delighted and praise him when he does.

● Hold him facing a mirror and point out what you both can see: "These are Joey's eyes." "This is Joey's nose." "This is Mommy's nose." Soon he will be pointing to his own nose on request, or finding the dolly's eyes or the teddy bear's ears.

to. Oh dear, you have a wet diaper. Poor baby, no wonder you've been crying. We'd better change you."

How do babies manage to do this? The answer is that, at first, he may not really break up the speech stream at all. It may just be a wash of interesting and engaging sounds that leave him feeling reassured and attended to. But as his listening skills improve, he begins to extract some important parts from the sounds he

is hearing and decode them by comparing them with the dictionary of words he is forming in his head. You give him clues by slowing your speech, exaggerating the boundaries between words, and speaking with expression and shifts of intonation.

Baby body language

Babies start to decipher what people around them mean by watching and listening, and what they understand

is made up of many different bits of information—what was said, who said it, when it was said, and where it was said. They learn that outstretched arms mean "Come here" long before they understand the words that go with the gesture. Although at first it may be difficult to know whether your baby has really understood the message, it's not long before he is using these familiar gestures himself at the

GETTING THE POINT
Now that he can point, he can direct your attention to what he desires most.

Checklist

Your baby's body language becomes increasingly expressive during his first year. He may:

- turns head away from the nipple (or spoon) when he has had enough
- jiggle his arms and legs when happy
- look from adult to toy then back
- tug at your clothing or arm
- hold objects out to you
- point
- touch the door to ask you to open it
- hold up his arms to be cuddled
- waves "bye-bye," shake his head to say "no," and nod to say "yes."

appropriate times. He knows that putting his arms out and smiling to you has a specific effect—he will be picked up and cuddled. Yet when a comparative stranger asks for a hug from your 10-month-old baby, he may shake his head vigorously— a gesture that is every bit as effective as verbal language.

Over the previous months, your baby has developed hand–eye coordination and can pick up and examine interesting objects within his reach. By nine months, your baby can follow your finger and look wherever you point. Now you have a useful tool for focusing his attention on interesting events and sights as well as the fascinating details in his picture books.

Roots of language

Your baby can direct your attention, too. At first, he will simply point— "I want it." However, by about 10 months, he will point at an object and then to you, and use his own sound for what he wants. The message here is different because it clearly shows he is aware that you know the word that he is using— "I know that you know what I mean." Here we have the roots of spoken language—"reference." Your baby is referring to the world around him. Without this simple shared reference, it would be almost impossible for him to learn language at all.

Gradually, babies begin to expect certain words in certain contexts and fix in their minds what they mean. By eight months your baby may follow simple instructions, especially if there is a visual cue such as "say bye-bye to Mommy" (plus wave), or "give it to Daddy" (plus an outstretched hand). He soon starts to show that he knows even more words, looking for the cat when it is mentioned in passing or picking up his cup when someone asks for a drink.

A social being

Toward the end of your baby's first year, you will have no doubt that he is fully equipped with almost everything he needs for effective communication:

● He can gesture welcome and rejection, imitate a full range of facial expressions, shout deep disapproval, and then change his tone to convey unrestrained joy.

● He enjoys dancing and romping, clapping games, music, and songs, and can produce a few magical little scales and tunes of his own.

● He will imitate some words if he can make the right sounds, but may still have no idea what they mean—

something an older sibling may take advantage of from time to time.

● He may also have one or two odd little words of his own, but often they can only be interpreted by people who know him very well.

In his first year, your baby has developed irresistible social skills alongside his language skills, and the two are now becoming enmeshed. He is discovering that speech is a very effective way of being sociable.

READY TO PLAY
Your baby is a more interesting playmate now that he has some social skills.

Expert tips

Start sharing books when your baby is about six months old.

● Choose simple board books with realistic pictures—they are easier for him to recognize than cartoons.

● Don't be put off if he wants to chew the book instead of look at it.

● Point and talk about what you see, but stop as soon as he loses interest.

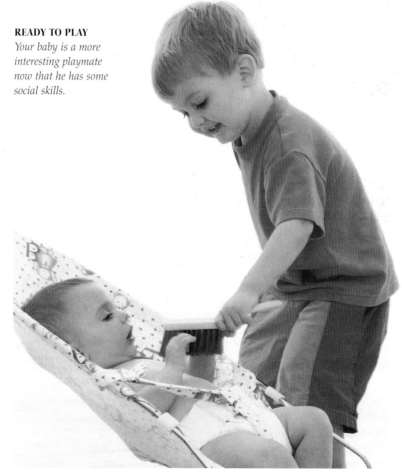

Talking with books

Books are a great way of interacting with your young child. Reading to her helps focus her attention precisely on words because she has pictures to refer to while she is hearing them. She will also love the attention, hugs, and close contact that go hand in hand with sharing a book.

● Just a few favorite books are all you need at first because your child will enjoy repetition as much as novelty. She is proud of what she knows and wants to share it repeatedly. Choose books with realistic, recognizable pictures that reflect your child's everyday experiences.She will enjoy joining in—lifting flaps to find hidden surprises and making animal noises in the right places.

● As a baby, your child may have simply pointed at the pictures, but now she is actively listening for words. Comment on what is happening on each page. Ask an occasional question—"What is the bear doing now?"— but not so many that it becomes a test; she will lose interest, especially if she is struggling to form words.

● By the age of two, children begin to enjoy books with a story and start to focus on sequences, and cause and effect. Tell the story in your own words—it will bring it to life. The more children hear people telling stories in their own voices, the more they want to do it themselves.

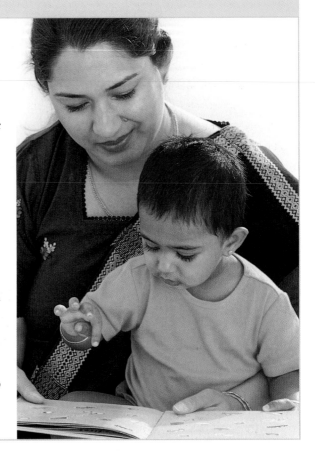

Golden rules

Adults often feel that they have to be in control of children to show them what's what, but this can lead to very dull interaction, with one party calling the shots and the other reacting. Spend time following the communication lead of your child. Begin by simply watching what she is doing; then venture a comment on some aspect of it: "You're putting the elephant in the truck now." Try to expand on her reply to extend her vocabulary and understanding. "The elephant's very big, isn't he? Do you think he's going to fit?" Don't try to distract your child from the focus of her attention—just go with the flow.

As an adult, it's very easy for you to anticipate your child's interests and needs and supply all the dialogue without her having to say much at all. She responds with a nod or shake of the head while you chatter on relentlessly. Make it a habit to listen carefully to her and be patient if you don't understand at first. Think of the effort she is putting into these first utterances and value them accordingly.

When she gets things wrong, it's because she has limited words at her disposal and is using what she has to elicit more information. Give her the correct word in a positive way instead of starting with a "no."

Avoiding baby talk

Perhaps one of the most important messages of this book is that you should be natural with your child. Although the parentese style of talk (see page 148) helps babies focus on language, some parents feel they need to go further and use a special vocabulary, too. Dogs become "bow-wows"; cats are "kitty-cats"; trains are "choo-choos" and cars are "vroom-vrooms." Baby talk like this is of no particular value, and must at times be puzzling for a child, particularly if she spends time in settings where everyone uses the correct words.

The only really useful baby words are your child's own—her first attempts at words based on what she can manage to say. For a while, a cushion may be a "pushin" because she can't quite produce a /k/ sound, or a fish, a "dit" until she can say /f/ and /sh/. However adorable you find these early versions of words, be happy to relinquish them as soon as she does. She shouldn't be made to feel that her baby pronunciation is so cute that it's something she needs to hold on to.

GOOD LISTENERS
Friends who listen with interest teach your child that her talk is important.

Expert tips

Try these 10 tips for keeping the conversation going:

- actively engage in your child's earliest communication

- listen carefully and value what she has to say

- follow her communication lead

- expand on what she says

- show that you are interested in what she has to say and that it is important to you

- be natural—don't use "baby language" or try to "teach" her how to speak

- engage in her play

- tell stories that she can understand

- give her confidence to keep on communicating

- help her speak to other people by translating any words she says that are hard to understand.

Useful contacts

UNITED STATES

GENERAL

The American Academy of Pediatrics
P.O. Box 927
Elk Grove Village, IL 60009
(847) 228-5005
www.aap.org

The American Medical Association
515 North State Street
Chigaco, IL 60610
(800) 621-8335
www.ama-assn.org

BabyCenter
www.babycenter.com
A wide range of pregnancy and parenting resources, including expert advice, live chats, message boards, and an online store

Bright Futures
Georgetown University
Box 571272
Washington, DC 20057-1272
(202)784-9556
www.brightfutures.org
Provides education and training for healthy mothers and babies

National Healthy Mothers, Healthy Babies Coalition
121 North Washington Street., Suite 300
Alexandria, VA 22314
(703) 836-6110
www.hmhb.org

BREASTFEEDING

Academy of Breastfeeding Medicine
191 Clarksville Road
Princeton Junction, NJ 08550
(877)836-9947 ext 25
www.bfmed.org

African–American Breastfeeding Alliance
940 Madison Ave.
Baltimore, MD 21201
(877)532-8535
www.aabaonline.com

The Center for Breastfeeding
The Healthy Children Project
327 Quaker Meeting House Rd,
Sandwich MA 02537
(508) 888-8044
www.healthychildren.cc

La Leche League International
1400 N. Meacham Rd.,
Schaumburg, IL 60173-4808
(800)LALECHE/525-3243
www.laleche.org

CRYING & COMFORTING

Colic Help
www.colichelp.com

International Association of Infant Massage
1891 Goodyear Avenue, Suite 622
Ventura, CA 93003
(805)644-8524, (805)644-7699
www.iaim-us.com

SLEEP

American SIDS Institute
(800)232-SIDS
2480 Windy Hill Road, Suite 380
Marietta GA 30067
www.sids.org

National Sudden Infant Death Syndrome Resource Center
2070 Chain Bridge Road, Suite 450
Vienna, VA 22182
(866) 866-7437
www.sidscenter.org

FEEDING YOUR BABY

American Dietetic Association
120 South Riverside Plaza, Suite 2000
Chicago, IL 60606-6995
(800)877-1600
www.eatright.org

Food and Nutrition Information Center
Agricultural Research Service, USDA
National Agricultural Library, Room 105
10301 Baltimore Avenue
Beltsville, MD 20705-2351
(301)504-5719
www.nal.usda.gov/fnic

National Institute of Child Health and Human Development
P.O. Box 3006
Rockville, MD 20847
(800)370-2943
www.nichd.nih.gov

Nutrition for Kids
www.nutritionforkids.com

BABY AND CHILD SAFETY

American College of Emergency Physicians (ACEP)
1125 Executive Circle
Irving, TX 75038-2522
(800)798-1822; www.acep.org

American Red Cross
2025 E Street NW
Washington, DC 20006
(866)GET-INFO; www.redcross.org

Centers for Disease Control and Prevention (CDC)
1600 Clifton Road
Atlanta, GA 30333
(888)232-3228; (800)311-3435
www.cdc.gov

National Center for Injury Prevention and Control

Mailstop K 65
4770 Buford Highway NE
Atlanta, GA 30341
(776)488-1506
www.cdc.gov/ncipc

US Department of Health and Human Services

200 Independence Avenue, SW
Washington, DC 20201
(877)696-6775
(202)619-0257
www.hhs.gov

World Health Organization (WHO)

WVI Liaison to WHO
World Vision International
18745 Sioux Drive
Spring Lake, MI 49456
www.who.int

LEARNING TO TALK

American Speech–Language–Hearing Association

10801 Rockville Pike
Rockville, MD 20852
(800)638-8255
www.asha.org

National Stuttering Association

119 W. 40th Street
14th floor
New York, NY 10018
(800) WE-STUTTER
www.nsastutter.org

Talking Point

www.talkingpoint.org
Offers advice on speech, language, and communication difficulties in children for parents, caregivers, and educational and health professionals

CANADA

GENERAL

Canadian Medical Association

1867 Alta Vista Drive
Ottawa, ON K1G 3Y6
(613) 731-9331
www.cma.ca

Canadian Paediatric Society

2204 Walkley Road
Suite 100
Ottawa, ON K1G 4GS
(613) 526-9397
www.cps.ca

BREASTFEEDING

La Leche League of Canada

Breastfeeding Referral Service
18C Industrial Drive
P.O. Box 29
Chesterville, ON K0C 1H0
(800) 665-4324
www.lalecheleaguecanada.ca

CRYING & COMFORTING

Parent Help Line

Kids Help Phone National Office
439 University Avenue
Suite 300
Toronto, ON M5G 1Y8
(416) 586-5437
www.parentsinfo.sympatico.ca

SLEEP

Canadian Foundation for the Study of Infant Death

586 Eglinton Avenue East
Suite 308
Toronto, ON M4P 1P2
(416) 488-3260
www.sidscanada.org

FEEDING YOUR BABY

National Institute of Nutrition

408 Queen Street
3rd Floor
Ottawa, ON K1R 5A7
(613) 235-7032
www.nin.ca

BABY & CHILD SAFETY

Safe Kids Canada

180 Dundas Street West
Toronto, ON
M5G 1Z8
(888) 723-3847
www.safekidscanada.ca

Canadian Red Cross

170 Metcalfe Street
Ottawa, ON K2P 2P2
(613) 740-1900
www.redcross.ca

LEARNING TO TALK

Canadian Association of Speech–Language Pathologists and Audiologists

401 – 200 Elgin Street
Ottawa, ON K2P 1L5
Tel: (800) 259-8519
www.caslpa.ca

Index

Acknowledgments

Senior editors Julia North, Salima Hirani
Senior art editor Hannah Moore
U.S. senior editor Jennifer Williams
Project editors Angela Baynham,
Anne Esden, Esther Ripley
Project art editors Claire Legemah,
Tracy Miles, Alison Tumer, Ann Burnham
Designer Iona Hoyle
DTP designer Julian Dams
Production controller Shwe Zin Win
Managing editor Liz Coghill
Managing art editors Emma Forge, Glenda Fisher
Photography art direction Sally Smallwood
Photography Ruth Jenkinson
Americanizer Christine Heilman
Publishing manager Anna Davidson

Publishing director Corinne Roberts

Text by Eileen Hayes, Tracey Godridge, Katy Holland,
James Law and Joanna Moorhead.

Dorling Kindersley would like to thank Alyson Lacewing
for proofreading and Sue Bosanko for the index.

Picture credits
Dorling Kindersley would like to thank the following for
their kind permission to reproduce their photographs:
10 Mother & Baby Picture Library, Ian Hooton (tr);
12 Mother & Baby Picture Library, Ruth Jenkinson (tl);
13 Bubbles, Angela Hampton (br); 28 Mother & Baby
Picture Library, Ruth Jenkinson; 67 Mother & Baby
Picture Library, Eddie Lawrence (t); 69 Mother & Baby
Picture Library, Ian Hooton (t); 132 Science Photo
Library: Mark Clarke (bl).

All other images © Dorling Kindersley.
For further information see: www.dkimages.com